Gods, Goddesses, and Mythology

VOLUME 5

Gorgons–Inanna

Marshall Cavendish
New York • London • Singapore

Marshall Cavendish
99 White Plains Road
Tarrytown, New York 10591

www.marshallcavendish.com

Library of Congress Cataloging-in-Publication Data

Gods, goddesses, and mythology/editor, C. Scott Littleton.
    p. cm.
    Includes bibliographical references and index.
    ISBN 0-7614-7559-1 (set : alk. paper)
1. Mythology--Encyclopedias. I. Littleton, C. Scott. II. Marshall
Cavendish Corporation. III. Title.

    BL312.G64 2005
    201'.3'03--dc22

2004040758

ISBN 0-7614-7559-1 (set)
ISBN 0-7614-7564-8 (vol. 5)

Printed and bound in China

09 08 07 06 05 04   6 5 4 3 2 1

General Editor
C. Scott Littleton, Occidental College, Los Angeles

Marshall Cavendish
Project Editor: Marian Armstrong
Editorial Director: Paul Bernabeo
Production Manager: Alan Tsai

Brown Reference Group
Project Editor: Chris King
Editors: Andrew Campbell, Sally MacEachern, Henry Russell,
  Lee Stacy
Designer: Steve Wilson
Picture Researcher: Helen Simm
Cartographer: Mark Walker
Indexer: Kay Ollerenshaw
Managing Editor: Tim Cooke

CONTENTS

GORGONS

In Greek myth the Gorgons were three monstrous sisters. The most famous of the trio was Medusa, whose snake-covered head was so frightful in appearance that people who looked upon it were turned to stone.

Above: The Head of Medusa *by Italian painter Caravaggio (1573–1610). Even after her head had been severed, Medusa's gaze could still turn people to stone.*

The Gorgons were triplets. Their mother and father, the sea deities Phorcys and Ceto, were also the parents of the Graeae, another set of female triplets who were born old and shared a single eye and tooth. According to Hesiod, the Greek poet of the eighth century BCE, two of the Gorgons, Stheno and Euryale, were "ageless and immortal." The third, more famous, sister was Medusa: she was mortal and met a violent end. Greek artists depicted the Gorgons as grotesque creatures with snakes for hair, and usually with fixed grins or screamlike expressions, boars' tusks, brazen hands, and golden wings.

In one version of the story, Medusa was originally a beautiful priestess who was working in the temple of Athena, the goddess of war and wisdom, when she was assaulted by Poseidon, the god of the sea. Athena was outraged by this act of sacrilege, but she lacked the power to attack Poseidon directly, so she took her revenge on him by transforming Medusa into a hideous Gorgon. According to a slightly different legend, Athena turned Medusa into a monster after the priestess had boasted that she was more beautiful than the goddess she served. This theme of pride going before a fall—hubris being eventually punished—occurs quite frequently in ancient Greek mythology.

The slaying of Medusa

Polydectes, king of the island of Seriphos, fell in love with a princess called Danae, but before he could marry her he wanted Perseus, her son by Zeus, out of the way. So he ordered the young hero to bring him the head of Medusa as a wedding present. The king thought that this was effectively a death sentence: the Gorgon would surely turn Perseus to stone.

Before Perseus could find Medusa, he first had to confront the Graeae, whose main task was to bar the road leading to their sisters the Gorgons. Perseus stole the Graeae's single eye and tooth and refused to return them until they told him the location of the Gorgons, which turned out to be in the far west, the place of the setting sun and the entrance to the underworld. The gods supplied Perseus with the other equipment he needed to complete his task. That included the cap of Hades, god of the underworld, which would make him invisible (*Hades* means "unseen"); the winged sandals of Hermes, the messenger of the gods; a purse known as a *kibisis* for carrying the Gorgon's head; and a scimitar, a curved sword.

Perseus used his winged sandals to fly over the ocean to the home of the Gorgons. On the advice of Athena, he approached Medusa backward, taking care not to look at the monster directly, but observing her reflection in his polished shield. Perseus decapitated Medusa as she slept, stuffed her head into the *kibisis,* and then, without ever looking at his prize, used his winged sandals and the cap of invisibility to escape the wrath of his victim's sisters, Stheno and Euryale. In one version of this myth, it was at this point that two children of Poseidon sprang fully formed

Above: This illustration by Philip van Gunst (18th century) shows Perseus slaying Medusa. Both the hero and his winged horse, Pegasus, avert their gaze from the monster, because to look at her is fatal.

from the blood that flowed from Medusa's neck. One was Pegasus, the winged horse; the other was Chrysaor, a giant with a golden sword.

Medusa's head was a powerful weapon for Perseus. When he fell in love with Andromeda and saved her from a sea monster, he turned her betrothed and his followers to stone so that he could marry her. He freed his mother, Danae, from the evil clutches of Polydectes, king of the island of Seriphos, by turning him and his followers to stone. He then made Polydectes' brother, Dictys, king. Perseus is also said to have used Medusa's head to turn Atlas to stone, thus easing the strain felt by the Titan who had been condemned to bear the weight of the heavens for eternity. Finally, Perseus gave Medusa's head to Athena, who placed it on her aegis (shield) or her breastplate as a symbol of her protective power.

Gorgons as symbols

The image of the Gorgon appears frequently in ancient Greek temples and on coins and vases. Most scholars believe that the likeness of the monster was intended to ward off evil. However, other interpretations exist. Some commentators have seen the Gorgon as a symbol of female energy: the face of Medusa depicts the scream of birth labor, while her power to turn people to stone represents the destructive capabilities of bad women. By placing the monster's head on her armor, Athena tames and harnesses the Gorgon's wild, elemental power.

KIRK SUMMERS

Bibliography

Garber, Marjorie, and Nancy J. Vickers, eds. *The Medusa Reader.* New York: Routledge, 2003.

Wilk, Stephen R. *Medusa: Solving the Mystery of the Gorgon.* New York: Oxford University Press, 2000.

SEE ALSO: Andromeda; Athena; Atlas; Danae; Hades; Harpies; Hermes; Perseus; Poseidon; Zeus.

GRACES

The Graces, known in Greek as the Charites and in Latin as the Gratiae, were the goddesses of beauty and graceful behavior. They had minor roles in a number of myths. Their embodiment of kindly manners and charm marks them as representations of the Greek ideal of womanhood.

There is a bewildering variety of information concerning the origins, names, and number of the Graces. Greek poet Hesiod (fl. 800 BCE) recorded that there were three Graces, born to the king of the Olympian gods, Zeus, and Eurynome, one of the Oceanids. The Oceanids were the offspring of the Titans Oceanus and Tethys. According to Hesiod, the Graces' names were Aglaea ("Splendor" or "Shining One"), Euphrosyne ("Joy" or "Gaiety"), and Thalia ("Festivity"). Greek travel writer Pausanias (143–176 CE), however, mentioned another source, which ascribes the goddesses' parentage to the sun god Helios and Aegle, one of the Hesperides, nymphs who guarded a tree bearing golden apples. This account of the Graces' origins would, at least, help explain Aglaea's name.

To confuse matters further, in his epic the *Iliad*, Greek poet Homer (c. 9th–8th cent. BCE) referred to a younger group of Graces, one of whom, Pasithea, he mentions by name. Homer's account suggests that he was aware of a younger and an elder group of Graces, a distinction that is reflected in a number of surviving Greek vase paintings, some of which depict five more Graces— Eudaimonia, Paidia, Pandaisia, Pannykhis, and Antheia. Other writers offer still further information. Greek poet Nonnus (fl. c. 450–470 CE) wrote that Pasithea was the daughter of Dionysus, god of wine, while Pausanias observed that the people of Sparta and Athens worshiped only two Graces. The Spartans called them Cleta ("Sound") and Phaenna ("Light"); the Athenians knew them as Auxo ("Increase") and Hegemone ("Queen").

Roles and relationships

The Graces personified beauty, charm, and grace, as well as acts of kindness or favor. The Greeks honored them in connection with social activities, such as banquets and dancing. In some accounts, the Graces were responsible for bestowing talents on mortals. Their attributes were very similar to those of the Muses, the nine goddesses who inspired artistic creativity, and Greek writers acknowledged this similarity. According to Hesiod, the Graces were the companions of the Muses and lived alongside them, together with Himeros, the personification of desire, on Mount Olympus. According to Hesiod, there were also similarities in the family backgrounds of the two groups of goddesses. Their mothers were both Titanesses or daughters of Titanesses, and their father was Zeus. The Greeks believed that Zeus's children—including the Graces, the Muses, the Fates, and the Seasons—provided humans with all they required to live ordered and moral lives.

The Greeks also associated the Graces with love and linked them with the goddess Aphrodite. References describe the Graces attending on Aphrodite as maidservants, reflecting their status as minor goddesses and Aphrodite's position as a major Olympian deity. During the Trojan War, Aphrodite, who fought on the side of Troy, was wounded in battle by the Greek warrior Diomedes. After this bruising encounter the goddess recovered her strength by putting on clothing made for her by the Graces.

Appearances in myth

A number of Greek myths include references to the Graces, but in general their involvement extended only as far as personifying charm and favor. To an extent, the Graces were similar to the Fates, the divine beings who determined the course of human lives. Both watched over the events of gods and mortals but were remote from them. Like the Fates, the Graces were present at the famous wedding of Peleus, king of Phthia, to the sea nymph Thetis, the first in a series of events that led to the Trojan War.

Right: Italian artist Sandro Botticelli (1445–1510) depicted the Graces, shown here in a detail from his painting Allegory of Spring. *Other deities appear in the complete painting, including Venus (Aphrodite), Cupid (Eros), and Mercury (Hermes), who appears here at left.*

Right: This 17th-century book illustration depicts the Three Graces being led by Mercury (Hermes).

The Graces also helped in the creation of Pandora, the first woman, who, according to Hesiod, unleashed strife on humanity. Hephaestus, god of metalworking, made Pandora out of clay; other deities gave her qualities that would make her attractive to her intended husband, Epimetheus, and the Graces adorned her with necklaces of gold.

Women in Greek Society

The Graces' charming and beautiful natures represented the ideal of femininity in ancient Greek society. In Classical-era Athens (479–338 BCE), for example, girls were educated at home and taught how to be good mothers and housewives. The Greeks believed that a woman's place was in the *kyrios* (home), while a man belonged in the *polis*, the public realms of politics, business, and warfare. The only exception to this rule was religion, where women could become priestesses and perform ceremonial rites at public assemblies. Some scholars argue that when Greek myths portray women as either powerful or aggressive, they represent men's fears about the opposite sex. When they depict women as demure and passive, they reflect men's fantasies about women, and the idealized form of feminine behavior. Mythical characters such as Hera, Athena, and Artemis, as well as the Harpies and the Gorgons, represent the powerful aspect of women; the Graces, the Muses, and the Hesperides are examples of the more passive side.

Greek poet Pindar (c. 522–c. 438 BCE) mentioned the Graces in connection with the myth of Ixion, the first mortal to kill a member of his own family. When Ixion went to Olympus so that Zeus could purify him for his misdeed, he fell in love with the Olympian ruler's wife, Hera. To test Ixion, Zeus made a cloud in the image of Hera. Fooled, Ixion slept with it, causing the cloud to give birth to Centaurus. Centaurus fathered the centaurs, who were part man and part horse. Pindar observed that the Graces did not honor the cloud's pregnancy, which suggests that childbirth was another area in which the goddesses played a role.

The Graces and marriage

The marriages of two of the Graces provide the stories with their greatest involvement in Greek myth. According to Hesiod, Aglaea married Hephaestus—although most other sources maintain that the blacksmith of the gods married the love goddess Aphrodite. In the *Iliad* Homer wrote that Hephaestus was married to one of the Graces. This relationship explains Homer's account of Hephaestus, whose mother Hera threw him out of Olympus when she realized he was lame. The god was rescued by Eurynome, the Graces' mother and, as a result, his mother-in-law. Another myth involves the younger Grace Pasithea, whom Hera offered to Hypnos, the god of sleep, as a bribe to ensure his help in putting Zeus to sleep. Hera wanted to help the Greeks in the Trojan War, but knew she had to do so without her husband's knowledge. Hypnos had sent the Olympian ruler to sleep once before, only for Zeus to find out and become enraged. Nevertheless, despite his fears, the god of sleep accepted Hera's offer because of his deep love for Pasithea.

Worship of the Graces

Pausanias records that the Graces were worshiped in Athens and Sparta, but notes that their most important shrine was in the town of Orchomenus in southern Greece. At the shrine people worshiped the Graces in the form of stones that they believed had fallen from heaven. Today it is widely accepted that these stones were meteorites. Orchomenus was home to a festival for the Graces, the Charitesea. Greek dramatist Aristophanes (c. 450– c. 388 BCE) mentions the Graces in connection with an Athenian festival, the Thesmophoria, in his play *Women at the Thesmophoria*. The festival, attended only by women, was held in honor of the fertility goddess Demeter and involved rituals promoting new life. According to Aristophanes, the participants prayed to the Graces, as well as to other deities, to ensure "that all may happen for the best at this gathering, both for the greatest advantage of Athens and for our own personal happiness."

Below: This sculpture of the Three Graces, by Italian Antonio Canova (1757–1822), is the most famous depiction of the deities from the early 19th century.

The Graces in art and literature

In ancient Greek vase paintings the Graces are often depicted nude and dancing in a circle. One vase, the *François Krater*, which dates from around 570 BCE, shows the Graces as attendants at the wedding of Peleus and Thetis. However, the goddesses inspired painters and sculptors long after the decline of ancient Greek and Roman cultures, most famously in a painting by Italian artist Sandro Botticelli (1445–1510) and as a sculpture by Antonio Canova (1757–1822), also Italian. Writers who have alluded to the Graces in their work include the English poets John Milton (1608–1674) and Edmund Spenser (1552–1599), who wrote about the deities in his long poem *The Faerie Queene*:

> These three on men all gracious gifts bestow
> Which deck the body or adorn the mind,
> To make them lovely or well-favored show;
> As comely carriage, entertainment kind,
> Sweet semblance, friendly offices that bind,
> And all the complements of courtesy.

ANDREW CAMPBELL

Bibliography

Guerber, H. A. *The Myths of Greece and Rome.* New York: Dover Publications, 1993.

Homer, and Robert Fagles, trans. *The Iliad.* New York: Penguin Books, 2003.

SEE ALSO: Aphrodite; Fates; Helios; Hephaestus; Hesperides; Muses; Oceanus; Pandora; Titans; Zeus.

GREAT SPIRIT

Native Americans traditionally believed in many spirit-entities, including the Great Spirit, the most powerful being in their pantheon. The Great Spirit was often depicted as the creator of the world and was sometimes associated with the sky, the heavens, or the sun.

Although people usually conceived the Great Spirit as being beyond physical reality, some Native American beliefs gave the being a variety of forms, including Old Man, Old Woman or Grandmother, Coyote, Rabbit or Hare, breath or air, and sun. Some peoples described the Great Spirit as a trickster deity, responsible for good and bad occurrences; other peoples envisaged the spirit as a pair of beings, such as twins or siblings or a husband and wife. Pairing the Great Spirit with a twin or sibling enabled people to explain the phenomena of good and evil, while pairing with a spouse helped explain the birth of humans. Most Native American peoples perceived the Great Spirit as a powerful neutral entity that assigned lesser spirits with particular duties—for instance, ensuring adequate rainfall or successful hunts.

Great Spirit, animals, and sacred objects

Stories involving the Great Spirit were usually creation myths, ones that explained the formation of the world and its inhabitants. These stories often involved other spirits, primeval animal entities, or sacred objects. In Crow mythology, primeval animal-spirits helped create the world. Only water existed until Old Man (the Great Spirit) saw two red-eyed ducks swimming in the world of water. Old Man sent Younger Duck to dive deep into the water, looking for the bottom. Younger Duck came up with a root. Old Man sent Elder Duck to find some earth. Elder Duck also dived deeply, and emerged with a ball of mud. Old Man put the root in the ball of wet earth, and blew on it three times. The ball grew until it formed a great land, inhabited by plants and animals. The story accounts for the fact that ducks live in water, on land, and in the sky. In Arapaho myth, Man-Above, a formless Great Spirit, created the world with the help of Flat Pipe, the Arapaho's most important sacred object. In the beginning there was only water, upon which Flat Pipe floated. Man-Above asked Flat Pipe to create a world, and Flat Pipe asked various water birds and animals to dive in search of earth. Duck, goose, swan, beaver, muskrat, and turtle all died trying to bring

Left: A Kiowa Native American participating in a Sun Dance ritual in the early 20th century. The Kiowa believed that the Great Spirit gave power to the Sun Dance, which encouraged natural growth and fertility.

Flat Pipe a piece of earth, but their deaths were not in vain. Flat Pipe combined the specks of mud on their bodies and created the world.

A sacred object of the Kiowa was Taime, a doll believed to possess *daw* (the power of the Great Spirit). A Kiowa tale relates how a Crow priest saw a poor Arapaho man praying to Taime before a Crow Sun Dance, a ritual designed to encourage natural growth and fertility. The priest gave the man the doll, which led to a change in his fortunes. He eventually married a Kiowa woman and happily lived among her people—Taime has remained in their descendants' possession ever since. Similar to the Christian concept of the Holy Spirit, Taime possessed *daw*, or power, and was part of Daw-Kee (literally "power man"; an older translation is "power thrown" or "throwing power"). Daw-Kee was synonymous with the Great Spirit, but while the Great Spirit was above all things, Daw-Kee was within everything. Taime symbolized the inherent power of the Sun Dance, but it also gave power to the ceremony—the Kiowa believed that without Taime, their Sun Dance would not result in fertility and regeneration.

The Algonquian-speaking Ojibwa's concept of the Great Spirit was similar to the Kiowa's. The Ojibwa believed in

Below: The coyote is common throughout the Great Plains, where it inspired many Native American myths.

Coyote and the Great Spirit

The figure of the coyote appears in many North American myths as the creator or as a messenger, hero, trickster, or fool. In some myths, Coyote-Creator met his animal counterpart, the coyote: they addressed each other as "elder brother" and "younger brother." Coyote was a transformer: sometimes he appeared as a handsome young man, at other times as an animal. Some myths present him as a sacred power, Great Spirit. According to the beliefs of the Crow and other Native Americans who traditionally lived on the Great Plains, Old Man Coyote impersonated the Creator by making people from a handful of mud and naming the buffalo, deer, elk, antelope, and bear. Some scholars believe Coyote's impersonation of the Creator was a mythic substitute, the result of a taboo against using the Great Spirit's name, which was too sacred to use except in special ceremonies.

Coyote's attributes were transformation, traveling, high deeds, and power. He changed river routes and mountain locations, created new landscapes, and obtained sacred objects for people. He also fought monsters: in Wasco tradition, for instance, Coyote defeated Thunderbird, killer of people. In some myths Coyote was a noble trickster. In one story, he took water from the Frog people so that the entire world could use it. In other myths, however, he was a harmful trickster, causing grief for animals and humans.

Gitchi Manito, a neutral Great Spirit that combined spirit, mystery, and magic. Manifestations of *pimadaziwin* (spiritual power) that came from an unknown source were attributed to Gitchi Manito. For the Ojibwa, *pimadaziwin* was crucial to life, and was invoked by shamans at Medwiwin ceremonies, which increased and distributed this spiritual force. Other Algonquian-speaking Native Americans recognized Michabo, the Great Spirit in the form of a hare. Michabo was associated with the sun and was the master of thunder and wind. In some accounts the morning star, Wabund Annung, was Michabo's wife; in other versions his wife was identified as Muskrat. Michabo and Muskrat created humans and were actively involved in human life.

Different concepts of the Great Spirit

Less directly involved in daily human life was Kishelemukong, the Great Spirit of the Leni-Lenape, or Delaware people. Kishelemukong was responsible for the origin of life-spirits known collectively as Manetuwak.

Below: According to the Shasta, Mount Shasta, in northern California, was the Great Spirit's tepee—the volcano's smoke came from the spirit's fire and rose through the tepee's smoke hole.

Manetuwak were involved with daily activities, and both men and women sought their guidance in ritualized prayers, visions, and dreams. Some Leni-Lenape identified the Great Spirit as Alowatsakima (meaning "Mighty Chief" or "Great Chief"), an allegorical entity. The Ute called their Great Spirit Pokoh ("Old Man"). According to Ute myth, Pokoh created the moon, who was good, and sun, who was bad. The sun, who was depicted as a man carrying a quiver of deadly arrows—the sun's rays—wished to kill all things because 20 men had killed his daughters, Venus and Mercury. After 50 days, Pokoh restored the sun's children to life so that he would not avenge their deaths. The Muskogee or Upper Creek Native Americans referred to their Great Spirit as Esaugetuh Emissee ("Master-of-Breath"). In their creation myth, Esaugetuh Emissee shaped the first humans from the clay of Nunne Chaha, the first hill to arise from the primeval waters.

The various Sioux peoples had many names for the Great Spirit. The Lakota (Eastern Sioux) named the Great Spirit Wakonda ("Power Above"), while for the Dakota (Midwest Sioux), Wakonda was the personification of an omnipresent, invisible life force. Other Sioux names for the Great Spirit were Nagi Tanka ("Great Spirit" or "Great

Mystery") and Taku Skanskan. Skan was the Dakota sky god who created the world and was the judge of the gods and of human souls.

The Sioux also referred to the Great Spirit as Wakan Tanka, a unifying life force that flowed in and through all things: flowers, wind, rocks, trees, birds, and animals. The same force breathed life into the first man—as a result, the human race enjoyed kinship with all creatures of earth, sky, and water. The Sioux believed that all creatures were of one blood, made by the same divine hand and filled with the essence of the Great Spirit. In their prayers and songs, the Sioux recognized the Great Spirit's work. They believed that they could avoid living in darkness by living close to nature and nature's ruler.

Caves, earth, and human creation

Many Native American peoples believed that they originally came from caves or the earth's core. The Muskogee, Seminole, Choctaw, Chickasaw, and Natchez, who in remote times were one confederacy, all recognized the hill, Nunne Chaha, as their point of origin. In myth, the house of their Great Spirit, Esaugetuh Emissee, was a cave in the center of Nunne Chaha, the first solid earth to arise from

the primeval waters. Esaugetuh Emissee made the first people from wet clay in his cave and raised a great wall upon which to dry them. The Awaxawi, one of the Hidatsa peoples, believed that they had lived inside the earth until First Creator and Lone Man competed to make the best country. Lone Man crossed the primeval water's surface and created the plains east of the Missouri River, while First Creator made the badlands to the west. The Awaxawi people climbed a vine to the surface; they wandered until they reached their present-day home in North Dakota.

The Zuni, one of the Pueblo peoples, called their Great Spirit Awonawilona ("All-father" or "Father Alone"). The Zuni believed that, at the beginning of time, there was nothing but darkness. Awonawilona thought outward into space, and created primeval mists. He made himself into the sun, the great father, and the darkness brightened with light. The mists thickened and became water. Awonawilona rested upon the waters and produced a green scum. The scum hardened and divided, becoming Awitelin Tsta (earth mother) and Apoyan Tachi (sky father). From these two beings sprang all life: mountains, clouds, rain, trees, corn, and stars. Awonawilona sent his sons, the Beloved Twain, into a mountain cave, where the first people and creatures

Above: A Sioux, photographed in 1908, offers a pipe to the Great Mystery, or Great Spirit. The buffalo skull on the ground symbolizes the spirit of the animal upon which the Sioux were dependent.

were living, lamenting their life in the sooty darkness. The Beloved Twain lifted Awonawilona into the skies, where he warmed the earth for all living creatures, and then cut the mountain with magic knives. The sons formed a ladder that led through five caves, which people and creatures used to climb to the earth's surface. The people split into six bands to become the ancestors of the six kinds of humans: yellow, tawny-gray, red, white, black, and mingled.

The impact of Christianity

The arrival of European settlers and Christianity in North America changed Native American beliefs. One myth that reflects this change involved Chareya ("Old Man Above"), the Great Spirit of the Shasta people. In the beginning, Chareya bored a hole in the sky with a large stone and pushed through masses of ice and snow, creating a great pyramid. The sun shone through the hole and melted some snow, creating streams and rivers. Chareya then climbed

down to the top of the pyramid and pushed his finger into the earth and planted the first trees. From the trees' leaves he made birds; from the branches he made fish and animals. Chareya feared his strongest creation, Grizzly, so he hollowed out the pyramid as a tepee, where he lived for thousands of snows. The Shasta knew he lived there because they saw smoke curling from the smoke hole of his tepee. According to the myth, when white men came, Chareya went away and no more smoke came from his tepee. This story not only reflects the impact of white settlers on Native American religion, but also serves as a creation account. Chareya's tepee was one name the Shasta gave to Mount Shasta, in northern California.

Christianity affected many Native American peoples' concept of the Great Spirit. After the arrival of the new religion, Ojibwa shamans began to say "Gitchi Manito [their Great Spirit] loves us" during traditional Medwiwin ceremonies. The Christian concept of love emanating from a supreme being reflected a change in belief: Gitchi Manito became a benevolent Great Spirit described as a father figure. Christianity also influenced the beliefs of the Awaxawi. Their spirit figure Lone Man took on attributes of Jesus Christ—his mother was a virgin, and he taught 12 men, who traveled with him and fought evil. The Sioux responded to Christianity in a different way. They thought that the Great Spirit could change Sioux beliefs to correspond with white ways if he wanted to do so, but maintained that he desired his red children to "believe and do differently" than his white children.

In the 19th and early 20th centuries, forced relocation and conversion to Christianity caused many Native Americans to relinquish their beliefs, and Great Spirit entities became associated with the Christian Holy Spirit. Early Christian missionaries did not allow Native Americans to equate God with any native deity or power, but they used the similarity of the concepts of a Holy Spirit and a Great Spirit in their attempts to convert them. This association allowed many Great Spirit beliefs to endure. The old ways were not completely forgotten, and today many Native American groups are revitalizing their traditional beliefs described in ancient myths.

ALYS CAVINESS

Bibliography

Hirschfelder, Arlene, and Paulette Molin. *Encyclopedia of Native American Religions*. New York: Checkmark Books, 2000.
Sullivan, Lawrence, ed. *Native Religions and Cultures of North America*. New York: Continuum, 2000.

SEE ALSO: Animals; Creation Myths; Native Americans; Shamans.

GREECE

The rich mythology of ancient Greece owes much to its mountains, caves, springs, and coastlines, which inspired a succession of people who settled in the region. Its great pantheon of deities dates from the classical period of Greek civilization, which peaked during the fifth century BCE with a great blossoming of arts, thought, and democracy.

During the New Stone Age, or Neolithic period (c. 9000–c. 3000 BCE), a rich civilization flourished in the small valleys and along the jagged coastline of mainland Greece. The region's mountainous terrain provided its inhabitants with security but left farmers only a handful of fertile valleys in which to work. A pattern therefore arose of small settlements isolated from each other by the mountains between. Many areas developed their own distinct cultures, and it was from these that Greek city-states later developed. The earliest inhabitants of Greece left artifacts but few more substantial traces. Consequently, today no one is sure where in mainland Greece they lived, and almost all that is known for certain about them is that they were not Greeks. The mysterious earliest inhabitants of the region are now known as Pelasgians.

Myths of the Stone Age

The earliest settled areas of Greece are thought to have been the plains of Thessaly and Macedonia in the north. They were productive agricultural regions, drained by rivers coursing from the mountains into the Aegean Sea. Like most Neolithic people across Europe, the Pelasgians probably built their houses on high ground near rivers. Their surroundings influenced their beliefs: springs and rivers were the homes of the earliest deities of the

Above: The mainland of Greece photographed from the air. The tallest peak is Mount Olympus, the mythological home of the ancient gods.

period. In particular, natural springs in limestone caves were sites for early ritual worship. Since agriculture was the dominant human activity, much of the earliest mythology was based on the worship of earth goddesses—feminine deities, almost invariably mothers, who provided humans with nourishment.

Greece

Left: This female figurine, carved between about 2800 and 2300 BCE, is typical of many found in the Cyclades.

The roots of the ancient Greek civilization that flourished during the classical period (479–338 BCE) may thus be traced back thousands of years to the Pelasgian period, when the dominant mythological figure was the bountiful mother goddess. The focal point of the earliest culture in Greece was the domestic hearth, where families would gather around the fire to recount and embellish existing myths, and no doubt from time to time invent new ones. Modern historians believe that these stories were sometimes accompanied by music and dance in a prehistoric form of drama. Eventually, the hearth itself became a sacred place—most houses and temples were built around fireplaces. By the classical period, the hearth had even obtained its own presiding deity, the goddess Hestia, who was worshiped by all.

Works of art dating from Stone Age Greece provide further evidence of mother-goddess worship. The Pelasgians created large-hipped figures of fertility goddesses from the plentiful limestone and marble of the mountain ranges. In the Cyclades, a group of islands in the Aegean Sea, archaeologists have discovered white statues of goddesses, which they believe were used in ritual burials. The statues, which have blank faces apart from long, stylized noses, and whose arms clutch their chests, date from Neolithic Greece. The figures are probably related to the small female objects of worship found at Stone Age sites throughout Europe, although their simple forms are unique to Greece.

In addition to mother-goddess statues, archaeological evidence from as early as 6500 BCE marks Greece as one of the original centers of Mediterranean civilization. Pottery discovered in the tells (large mounds of rubbish on a long-settled site) of Thessaly and Macedonia shows the beginning of a ceramic tradition that would, much later, become influential throughout the ancient world.

Bronze Age Greece

During the Bronze Age in Greece (c. 3000–c. 1200 BCE), an era known as the Helladic period, an influx of settlers arrived from Anatolia (part of modern Turkey). Along with their expertise in making bronze (an alloy of copper and tin), these immigrants brought their own mythology. Yet although their religious beliefs and practices were not the same as those of the Pelasgians, the powers and responsibilities of their deities would not have been unfamiliar to those who already lived in Greece. For example, the inhabitants of Çatalhüyük, a Stone Age settlement in south-central Anatolia (c. 6700–c. 5650 BCE), worshiped an all-powerful goddess figure. The Anatolians had also been influenced by trade contact with the people of the Indus Valley on the modern border between Pakistan and India: anthropologists have thus been able to trace links between the cultures of ancient civilizations stretching from south-central Asia to Greece, and later to Rome and northern Europe.

The goddess worship of all these ancient peoples fed a common mythology that was based on the figure of a great mother, the creator and destroyer of life, whose devotees sought help in this life and rebirth in the next. Greek myths written down centuries later show remnants of these prehistoric themes and concerns. For example, the myth of the agricultural goddess Demeter, whose grief at the loss of her daughter, Persephone, made the earth barren, demonstrates the themes of transformation and fertility that would have been central to the beliefs of Stone Age and Bronze Age Greece.

The age of invasions

Between around 1900 and 1500 BCE, a series of invasions by Indo-European speakers, cousins of the Arya who invaded northern India at about the same time, gradually eclipsed the earlier goddess civilizations of ancient Europe. From the north of the Danube River, which flows east from modern Germany to the Black Sea, tribes descended on settlements in Greece. The first to arrive were the Achaeans, who swept down from the hills on horse-drawn chariots, which the natives were powerless to resist. The Achaeans introduced potter's wheels and a new style of architecture that featured megarons—

rectangular rooms with a central hearth. Over the next four centuries, mainland Greece endured further waves of invasion by other Indo-European-speaking groups, including the Dorians from the northwest, the Aeolians from the east, and the Ionians from Anatolia. Gradually all the invading peoples merged with the Pelasgians to form a society with its own distinctively Greek identity.

The new mythology that the invaders introduced to Greece was based on a belief in sky gods. The cloud-capped Mount Olympus, in the northeast of the country, became the home of such deities.

Right: This carving from the fourth century BCE is the head of Demeter, the Greek goddess of agriculture.

Forms of Worship

The ancient Greeks worshiped their gods in much less formal and structured ways than the adherents of most modern religions. They had no religious dogma (a set of beliefs that had to be accepted as a condition of entry). There was no insistence on a link between religion and morality, and no suggestion that human happiness in the next life was conditional on good behavior in this.

Most acts of collective worship took the form of open-air processions, often with a musical accompaniment, to the altar of the god, where sacrifices were carried out. Attendance was normally optional: Greeks were free to perform their own sacrifices privately if they wished. Priests might attend a ritual, but their presence was not essential. Each city had its own tutelary spirit, a special deity who looked after the state and was particularly venerated by its inhabitants: at Athens it was Athena; at Corinth, Poseidon.

Later, however, some Greek myths—particularly those that concerned Zeus's wildest exploits—came under scrutiny by philosophers, who contended that anything the chief god did must, by definition, be good. By the fifth century BCE, Zeus had therefore stopped philandering and become the model of rectitude and the upholder of justice. The awe in which he came to be held is clear in contemporary art and literature.

Left: The Tholos at Delphi was built in the fourth century BCE. It may have been a shrine to the earth goddess Gaia.

None of the cultures was dominant; they all intermingled to produce a richly cosmopolitan mixture of traditions from contrasting areas of Europe and Asia.

Although, in general, very little is known about the Pelasgians, there are several identifiable links between their mother-goddess culture and Achaean religious practices. For example, Rhea was the name given by the Pelasgians to the "great mother" deity. In recognition of her status, the Achaeans acknowledged her as the mother of Zeus, chief of the Olympian gods. Similarly, the Achaeans believed that Zeus's birthplace was in a cave on Mount Dicte in Crete, which suggests that they incorporated the earlier Pelasgian belief in caves as sacred sites, where worshipers took part in ritual practices.

"Dark-age" Greece

So little is known of the next period of Greek history, from around 1500 to 900 BCE, that scholars refer to it as a dark age. The exploits of Dorian and Achaean heroes in this era form the basis of much Greek mythology, and also provide some insight into historical events. The story of Theseus

Other landscapes in Greece also inspired and influenced the new mythology. To the Achaeans, as well as to the Dorians and other peoples, the region's dense forests and mountain springs were home to unknown dangers and deities, while for many of the invaders the sea was an entirely new and strange phenomenon that became another rich source for mythology.

Yet in parallel with these innovations, Achaean mythology assimilated many aspects of the mother-goddess beliefs of the original inhabitants of Greece. This was at least partly because the invaders interbred with the earlier inhabitants, rather than expelling or eradicating them.

and the Minotaur, for example, probably reflects the Achaeans' real-life conquest of the Mediterranean island of Crete. Theseus was a hero from Athens who ended the tribute his city had once paid to King Minos of Crete. The remains of an intricate Minoan palace at Knossos suggest the kind of labyrinth that might have given rise to the myth of the Minotaur, half-man and half-bull, whom Theseus had to seek out in the mazelike halls of Knossos.

The story of the Trojan War also seems to be a semifictional account of real events. The *Iliad*, the epic by Greek poet Homer (c. ninth–eighth century BCE), recounts the adventures of the dark-age heroes Agamemnon, king of Mycenae, and his brother Menelaus, king of Sparta, who collaborated in recovering Helen, wife of Menelaus, after she had been abducted by the Trojan prince Paris. The legend probably reflects the real battles between the seafaring people of Troy in western Asia and the up-and-coming Achaeans, who wanted to control the trade routes between the Black Sea and the Mediterranean.

Archaeological excavations at Mycenae, where Agamemnon may have been buried, give a few clues to the cultural shift that occurred during the dark age. The language of the Achaeans and other tribes was a precursor of ancient Greek, and the Achaeans' patriarchal customs helped to significantly change the Bronze Age culture in Greece. Instead of a partnership between males and females, a new order emerged in which the supreme leaders were always men—chiefs or kings, priests or judges.

Classical Greece

During the eighth and seventh centuries BCE, the Greeks started to establish city-states at home and to colonize new territories in Turkey, North Africa, Sicily, and Italy, as well as on the islands of the Aegean Sea, including Thasos, Lemnos, Lesbos, Scyros, and Rhodes.

Historically, one of the most important places colonized by the Greeks was Ionia, a coastal strip in western Asia Minor (part of modern Turkey), measuring up to 30 miles (48 km) wide and about 90 miles (145 km) long, and extending from the Hermus (now Gediz) River in the north to beyond the Miletus peninsula. For many years the Ionians had mixed with the ancient Pelasgians, but after the Dorian invasion they fled the mainland. Ionian ships ventured into the Aegean Sea and gradually took control of it from the Phoenicians, a trading people who had settled throughout the Mediterranean. The Ionians' dominance of the Aegean allowed their culture to spread back to Greece, where it became influential. Homer himself was said to have been an Ionian Greek.

Right: This gold burial mask was excavated at Mycenae, the most important center of civilization on mainland Greece during the Late Bronze Age (c. 1600–c. 1000 BCE).

The founding of Athens

The Greeks established a distinctive political organization, the city-state, both on mainland Greece and in the territories they colonized. Each of the city-states was fiercely independent, although at times they formed alliances against a common enemy—for example, according to the *Iliad*, the city-states of Sparta, Athens, Thebes, and Argos joined forces during the Trojan War. Greek city-states shared a common religion and language, but had many different forms of political organization, from dictatorships to rule by small groups of wealthy people to rule by a system that can be seen as a precursor to modern democracy. Athens is the city-state about which we have the most information. It was founded on the plain of Attica in southeastern Greece, and during the fifth century BCE it was the most powerful city-state. The Athenians' mythological explanation for the founding of their city relates how Athena, the virgin goddess of arts, crafts, and war, battled the sea god Poseidon to win Attica. The myth implies that the inhabitants of the region had previously regarded Poseidon as their patron, but then switched their allegiance to Athena.

Athena's totems (sacred objects), the owl and the serpent, indicate that she may have first been worshiped

The Acropolis

In classical Greece every important urban center of population had an acropolis, or "uppermost city." The acropolis was the highest and most defensible part of the settlement. On it were built temples, treasuries, and other important civic buildings.

The best-known acropolis is that of Athens, the capital of modern Greece. There the ancient Greeks built one of the finest groups of temples in the ancient world, first settled during the Neolithic Period. By the Bronze Age (c. 3000 BCE) it was occupied by a royal palace and an array of houses. The surviving structures date from an extensive building program initiated by the statesman Pericles in the fifth century BCE. The major monuments on the Athenian Acropolis are the Parthenon (the temple of Athena Parthenos), the Propylaea (gateway), the temple of Athena Nike (goddess of victory), and the Erechtheum (the temple of Athena and Erechtheus).

Below: Now a UNESCO World Heritage Site, the Acropolis has dominated the Athens skyline for 2,500 years.

by the Minoan civilization (c. 3000–c. 1100 BCE). Having adopted her, the Greeks gave her a more warlike spirit. The Athenians saw her as the daughter of Zeus. By worshiping her, they hoped that they would also be protected by the king of the gods. According to myth, Athena's mother was the sea nymph Metis. When Metis was pregnant with Athena, Zeus was warned that her second child would overthrow him. He therefore swallowed his wife, but later regretted his action and arranged for either the Titan Prometheus or the god Hephaestus to split his head open with an ax. Athena emerged from Zeus's head. Athenians regarded their patron as a symbol of divine intelligence because of the method of her birth. Moreover, since she was a motherless virgin, the worship of Athena by the Athenians provides another link between the belief in sky gods and the mother-goddess worship of earlier Greece.

Yet another link to ancient mother-goddess worship can be detected in the mythical first ruler of Athens, Cecrops, whose title was Autochthonus, or "born of the earth." Cecrops—a half-human, half-snake Egyptian deity believed to have ruled Athens in the 16th century BCE—reflects the strong influence of Egypt on early Greece. This influence can also be seen in the myth of Demeter, whose search for her lost daughter, Persephone, echoed that of the Egyptian mother-goddess Isis for her dismembered husband, Osiris, after he was murdered by his brother Seth. As the Romans later thought of themselves as taking the torch of civilization from the Greeks, so the Greeks had taken it from Egypt and the mother-goddess culture of western Asia. Having inherited the wisdom and arts of Crete, Egypt, and Asia, the Athenians forged them into their own distinctive culture.

Athens, democracy, and the gods

Despite the imaginative power and creative genius of Athenian mythology, literature, sculpture, and architecture, even the greatest works in these forms were stylized continuations of established traditions. In the sphere of politics, however, Athens developed a form of government that was without precedent in history, and which later became important throughout the world. The innovation was democracy: Greek laws were not made by decree, as was the almost universal practice in other parts of the ancient world, but by a process that involved some of the people and had to be sanctioned by philosophers in consultation with the gods. Many commentators have

Right: This bronze statue of the goddess Athena wearing a crested helmet dates from around 375 BCE.

597

pointed out that ancient Athenian democracy was not the same as modern democracy. It gave little voice to the majority of citizens. However, others argue that the Athenian example provided the foundation on which was later built the modern democratic practice of one person, one vote.

At the center of every Greek society was the polis, which came to mean "city" but in its original usage would best be rendered in English as "the house on the hill," or the place where the chief lived. By the seventh century BCE, the chief or king had lost much of his power to his army officers, and this development sowed the seeds for classical Greek democracy in the fourth century BCE.

The laws that made Athens great were the work of Solon (c. 630–c. 560 BCE), an aristocrat whom the Athenians elected as their dictator. Solon's laws emphasized justice and fairness. The poor were no longer enslaved for debt. The size of landed estates was limited by law, and high office was based on wealth alone, not birth. Athens remained an aristocracy, and ordinary wage-earners could not hold political office, but at least they could debate and vote in the popular assembly, from which justices were drawn for the courts of law. In Solon's poems to Zeus, he likened his reforms to the lavish bounty of the ancient mother goddess, thus rooting Athenian government in both the prehistoric earth religions and the sky gods.

Athens's main rival was Sparta, a city-state in the Peloponnese in southern Greece. Unlike other city-states, which established colonies in other parts of the Mediterranean, the Spartans conquered other Greeks. Sparta became the most powerful city-state in Greece, but it was plagued by problems. Its conquered territories, such as Messenia, were almost constantly rebellious, and the cost of keeping them subjugated was high. At home, poor Spartans rioted against the handful of rich families who owned most of the land. Meanwhile, the rival city-state of Athens grew in wealth and prestige, largely through foreign trade. The land-based, wealthy aristocracy of Sparta had come to a political and economic dead end. Their ideal of the Achilles-like hero, mighty in war but foolish in practical matters, was rapidly becoming outmoded. Instead, the Athenian ideal, represented by clever, innovative heroes such as Theseus and Odysseus, was destined to prevail.

Mythology in classical Greece

During the classical period and beyond, Greek thinkers, writers, and artists interpreted myths in order to reflect on human nature. In dramas, playwrights such as Euripides (c. 486–c. 406 BCE) and Sophocles (c. 496–406 BCE) shaped

The 12 Great Olympian Gods

Aphrodite:	Goddess of love and beauty.
Apollo:	God of prophecy, music, and the arts; also associated with the sun.
Ares:	God of war.
Artemis:	Goddess of hunting and protector of women during childbirth.
Athena:	Goddess of war, wisdom, and domestic crafts.
Demeter:	Goddess of corn and agriculture.
Dionysus:	God of wine and ecstasy.
Hephaestus:	God of fire and metalworking.
Hera:	Goddess of marriage and childbirth and queen of the gods.
Hermes:	Herald and messenger of the gods.
Poseidon:	God of the sea.
Zeus:	God of rain and thunder and king of the gods.

myths into plays known as tragedies. The paradox of a beautiful human form fated to wind up in the dark underworld of Hades is at the core of both Greek mythology and tragedy. Central to tragic drama was hubris, the pride that goes before a fall. That pride is the hamartia, or tragic flaw, of humanity. The Greeks believed that three sisters known as the Moirai (Fates) pursued each individual from birth to death. According to the account in the *Theogony* of Hesiod (fl. 800 BCE), Clotho spun the thread of life; Lachesis measured this thread, apportioning good or bad luck to each person; and Atropos cut the thread. Later writers raised Nemesis to divine status as the goddess of retribution, thus diminishing the role of the Fates.

While the mother goddess was still worshiped by some, the ascendancy of masculine gods in Greek mythology reinforced the dominant role of men in society. Women in Athens were confined to hearth and home, while men were educated, ran the state, and could even decide whether their children lived or died. The control of males over marriage, paternity decisions, and property was absolute. Reason was regarded as a male principle, and it was represented by Apollo, the sun god whose lyre symbolized poetry and music and the harmony between the mind and the body.

A counterbalance to Apollo was Dionysus, the god of wine and ecstasy. First worshiped in Thrace and Phrygia, he was another Greek god with exotic origins. He was associated with the wilderness and drew his devotees, usually females, into the mountains and forests to worship him in wild ceremonies that echoed ancient mother-goddess rituals. Dionysus inspired passion and excess, not reason.

Above: *This painting by Italian artist Cecchino Salviati (1510–1563) depicts the three Fates—Clotho, Lachesis, and Atropos.*

The influence and impact of Greek mythology

Mythology is an essential element of civilization, but most ancient myths fell into disuse as the society that devised them progressed or disintegrated. Greek myths were different. They spread first to Italy, where they were taken up by the Romans, whose own gods had less clearly defined personalities than those of the Greeks. Roman writers were therefore pleased to be able to invest their deities with biographical backgrounds and characters that came "ready-made" from an earlier culture.

Rome then conquered the greater part of Europe, and ruled it for over 500 years, from the first century BCE to 476 CE. They stamped the imprint of their culture firmly on occupied territories from Iberia to the Black Sea, and much of that culture was of Greek origin. As a result, Western culture is heavily indebted, albeit indirectly, to ancient Greece. Examples of Greek cultural influence are everywhere. The fibrous cord that connects the muscles of the human calf to the heel bone is known as the Achilles tendon, after the Greek hero whose fatal flaw was in that part of his body. One of the psychological fixations identified by Sigmund Freud is named after Oedipus, the son of Laius, king of Thebes. In English and many other European languages, map books are known as atlases, after the Titan who held the heavens on his shoulders. A good-looking man is known as an Adonis. A Caribbean ballad or dance with a certain rhythm is named after Calypso, the sea nymph who detained Odysseus for seven years in Homer's *Odyssey*.

Above: Part of a fresco by Italian Antonio Maria Viani (c. 1555– c. 1632), this detail shows the chariot of the sun being driven by Apollo.

However, the culture of ancient Greece survives in more than just a host of names and expressions. The Greek city-states of the classical era made important and lasting contributions to art, architecture, literature, mathematics, religion, philosophy, and education in the West and in all the countries that were subsequently colonized by Europeans. Above all, ancient Greece is looked on as the inspiration for our modern theories of democracy. Because ancient Greece is still alive in these important ways, its mythology—though long superseded by monotheistic religions or no religion at all—has retained a significant role in the modern consciousness. That is why its echo (a Greek nymph) can be heard daily in modern life, while the cultures of the ancient Egyptians and Hittites, for example, are now largely confined to museums and school textbooks.

BARBARA GARDNER

Bibliography
Graves, Robert. *The Greek Myths*. New York: Penguin USA, 2003.

Howatson, M. C., and Ian Chilvers. *Concise Oxford Companion to Classical Literature*. New York: Oxford University Press, 1993.

SEE ALSO: Agamemnon; Apollo; Athena; Demeter; Dionysus; Fates; Helen; Hestia; Isis; Menelaus; Muses; Odysseus; Osiris; Paris; Persephone; Poseidon; Prometheus; Theseus; Zeus.

HADES

Hades, whose name means "the unseen," was the brother of Zeus, king of the Greek gods. He was the ruler of the underworld, the home of dead spirits, a role that gave him his other name, Polydegmon, "host of many guests." As well as a god, Hades was also the place of the dead, a realm that Greek poet Homer (c. ninth–eighth century BCE) described as being cloaked in mist and cloud.

Hades' early life was marked by abuse and suffering. His father, Cronus, was the son of the sky god Uranus and the earth goddess Gaia. Cronus castrated his father in order to gain supreme power for himself. However, a seer told Cronus that one of his sons would be the death of him. Ignoring the protests of his sister and wife Rhea, Cronus swallowed all their children as they were born. Finally, Rhea deceived her husband when she gave him a stone swaddled in cloth instead of Zeus, her youngest child. The boy was spirited away to a cave in the middle of Crete. When Zeus

Below: A medieval depiction of Hades and Persephone—the king and queen of the underworld—seated inside the mouth of an owl, a symbol of death. At their feet lies the dog Cerberus.

Left: Proserpina *(1877) by English painter Dante Gabriel Rossetti (1828–1882). In myth, Hades abducted Proserpina (the Latin name for Persephone) and forced her to become queen of the underworld.*

matured, he forced Cronus to vomit up his brothers and sisters: Poseidon, Hades, Hera, Hestia, and Demeter. Working together, the young deities overcame their father and banished him to a distant place.

After deposing Cronus, Hades and his two brothers cast lots for the kingdoms they would rule. Zeus won the heavens and Poseidon won the sea, which left the underworld for Hades. While the gods and goddesses of Olympus frolicked and celebrated, Hades' job was to govern the world of the dead.

The abduction of Persephone

Unlike the other gods, Hades was not known for his many romances. The exception was his love for the beautiful young Persephone, daughter of Demeter, the goddess of fertility and corn. Unknown to Persephone and her mother, Hades had asked Zeus for permission to marry the girl. Zeus agreed, perhaps because he felt guilty about having won a kingdom so much more agreeable than his brother's. Meanwhile, Gaia had planted a narcissus flower in honor of her grandson Hades. She wanted to please the god of death and left him this token of her esteem. Persephone, playing in a meadow with her friends, came upon the flower and was transfixed by it. As she picked it, Hades rose out of the ground in a chariot pulled by black stallions and grabbed the girl. The chariot sped into a dark chasm, which the earth then closed over without a trace.

Demeter sought anxiously for her daughter. She asked all the gods and goddesses if they could tell her where she was, but no one knew. Only the goddess Hecate, who lived in an underworld cave, and the sun god Helios, who served as a lookout for the gods, had heard Persephone's cries. On the 10th day of her search, Demeter learned from Hecate what had happened to her daughter. Hecate led the grieving mother to Helios, who told her that Zeus had given Persephone to Hades, Demeter's own brother.

Demeter was no stranger to the underworld. As a vegetation deity, she went underground during the winter. She was known to the Athenians as the soil in which the dead, called "Demeter's people," were buried. In their own right, and not only through Hades, both she and Persephone were connected with the realm of the dead, and the identities of the three deities mingle in myth. However, Demeter objected furiously to Zeus's agreement that Hades could marry her daughter.

Both mother and daughter pined at their loss of each other and refused to eat. Because Demeter would not help the crops grow, the earth became barren and people starved. For her part, Persephone sulked and ignored Hades, refusing to be queen of the underworld. She wanted to be with her mother and nothing could console her. In a weak moment, she accepted a handful of pomegranate seeds from Hades, unaware that he was tricking her into permanent residence in the realm of the dead. Once any food was tasted there, the one who had eaten could never leave. Finally, Demeter insisted that Zeus arbitrate the dispute. The Olympian ruler agreed, fearful that the people of earth would starve to death.

Demeter accused Zeus of plotting with Hades to abduct her beloved daughter. Hades said that Persephone had eaten the fruit of the underworld and was now his forever. Persephone looked from mother to husband, wringing her hands. She missed Demeter but had come to love the dark, romantic Hades. To begin with, Zeus wanted to allow Persephone to choose where she lived. If she rejected Hades, she could go home to her mother. Although Persephone wanted to be with Demeter, she felt that she now belonged with Hades.

In the end, Zeus had to make the decision himself. He ruled that Persephone should live with her mother in the spring and summer; for the rest of the year, when crops did not grow, she would live with Hades. She therefore became queen of the underworld and lived in the realms of both the living and the dead. Hades proved to be a faithful husband, except for his attempts to seduce the nymphs Leuce and Menthe. Persephone was so angry at Hades' behavior that she turned Leuce into a poplar tree and Menthe into a mint plant. Hades seems to have been abashed by this retaliation, since he did not stray again.

Hades, Theseus, and Peirithous

The myth of Peirithous is closely linked to Hades' marriage to Persephone. Peirithous was a king of a people called the Lapiths, who became the companions of Theseus, the Greek hero and king of Athens. According to the story, both men vowed to marry daughters of Zeus. Theseus chose Helen of Sparta—who was later rescued by her brothers—while Peirithous chose Persephone. The pair traveled down to the underworld and informed Hades of their aim. The god calmly invited both of them to sit

down, which they did, not realizing until it was too late that they had sat on chairs of forgetfulness, from which they could not get up. Some time later, the hero Heracles came to the underworld to fetch the dog Cerberus as the last of his 12 Labors. Heracles was able to rescue Theseus from his seat, but not Peirithous—when he tried to move him, the ground trembled. As a result, Peirithous remained forever a prisoner in the underworld.

Right: The Rape of Proserpina *(1621–1622), by Italian sculptor Gian Lorenzo Bernini (1598–1680), depicts Hades abducting his future bride.*

Above: This Greek vase painting from around 330 BCE depicts Hades, the king of the underworld, with his queen, Persephone. At first Persephone resisted her marriage to Hades. However, she later became jealous of her husband's attempted affairs.

The Journey to the Underworld

When a Greek or Roman died, a coin was put over each eye of the body or in its mouth. People performed this custom in the belief that the dead souls had to pay Charon, the surly ferryman who carried the dead across the Styx River. Roman poet Virgil (70–19 BCE) described Charon as "frightful and foul, his chin covered with unkempt hoary hair, his fierce eyes lit with fire, and a filthy cloak hanging from a knot on his shoulder." If the dead had no money, they were doomed to remain forever on the shore of the black, subterranean river.

When those who did have coins reached the other side of the river, the god Hermes—known to the Romans as Mercury—guided the souls to their new home. The three-headed watchdog Cerberus (see box, page 607) allowed the dead to enter the gates of the underworld, but he refused to let them pass back out again. Several places in ancient Greece were believed to be entrances to Hades, including the Alcyonian Lake in the northern Peleponnese and Taenarum in the southern Peleponnese.

Right: A Roman relief sculpture of Charon ferrying the dead across the Styx River. The relief, carved on a sarcophagus, represents the journey that awaited the soul of the body inside.

Greek views of Hades

Hades' character was harder to define than that of other gods, although there are parallels between him and several different deities. Like Hermes, the divine messenger, Hades possessed a helmet of invisibility. The personalities of both gods involved elements of trickery and concealment. Hades had a stern, unemotional manner, which made him seem lacking in personality. However, he could be moved to compassion: after the musician Orpheus played his lyre in the underworld, Hades agreed that his dead wife, the nymph Eurydice, could return with him to the world of the living. However, Orpheus could not meet the condition that he could not look at his wife until they had returned home, and he lost Eurydice forever.

Hades also had a passionate side and was sometimes regarded as an aspect of Dionysus, the god of wine. This parallel suggests that Hades, or the underworld, was more than the realm of the dead; it was also a place visited by the living, whether in sexual ecstasy, drunkenness, or mystical bliss. The Greeks also believed that they could journey to Hades during their dreams, or when they suffered from depression. Awareness of both Hades, who ruled the world of shadows, and Zeus, who ruled the world of light, provided people with a deeper sense of the meaning of life.

Unlike gods of the underworld in many other cultures, Hades was not considered evil. However, the Greeks did generally fear and shun him. It was customary for Greeks to avert their eyes when his name was mentioned and to identify him with Plutus, the god of wealth, in order to stay on his good side. Sometimes the Greeks saw Hades as the alter ego of Zeus and called him Zeus-Chthonios, a title that reinforced Hades' earthy qualities since chthonian deities were associated with both the dead and the fertility of the earth. The linking of Hades to more benign deities may have represented an attempt by the Greeks to harmonize dying with living. However, most Greeks did not make sacrifices to Hades because it did no good to plead with death. No hymns were sung to him, and few images of the god exist in Greek art. Hades was a hidden deity, perhaps because people feared that acknowledging his presence would draw them into the void with him.

Other inhabitants of Hades

Other beings also lived in the underworld, including the Furies, or Erinyes, who pursued those who sinned against members of their own family, and Hecate, a deity who bridged the world between living and dead, who had her own cave. The Furies sprang up from drops of blood shed when Cronus castrated his father, Uranus. These fearsome spirits carried serpents in their hands and were hideously ugly. The Athenians, who called them the Eumenides ("kindly ones"), worked hard to appease them lest they destroy Athens in retribution for the crime of Orestes, who had murdered his mother, Clytemnestra. Hades himself did not torture the guilty dead: he left the task to the Furies.

The judges of the dead were Minos, Rhadamanthys, and Aeacus, the gatekeeper. Hades remained hidden from the process of pronouncing judgment on the dead, although it is not clear what effect this judgment had, since those who were punished in the underworld had already been condemned by the gods. There were five rivers in the underworld: the Styx, the river of hate; the Acheron, the river of sorrow; the Lethe, the river of forgetting; the Cocytus, the river of cries; and the Phlegethon, the river of fire. Each river represented an aspect of the death process, such as anger, grief, or surrender. The sections of Hades, therefore, were not just geographical locations, but states of mind or soul.

Changing beliefs about the underworld

Across Europe during the Stone Age, people had seen the underworld as the home of the Great Mother and, as a result, a place of rebirth. Prehistoric sites like the Hypogeum in Malta allowed living worshipers to mingle with their dead. In Çatalhüyük, in central Turkey, where a peaceful civilization flourished in the fifth millennium BCE, dead family members were often buried under the beds of their living kin, indicating that death was not to be dreaded. However, by the time of the Sumerian empire in Mesopotamia (c. 3000–c. 1900 BCE), the underworld had become a much more negative place. The Sumerians believed it was situated beneath Apsu, a deity and also

Left: Engraving of a sculpture of Hades by English artist Charles Grignion (1717–1810). Hades holds his two-pronged staff, which the Greeks believed he used to drive spirits into the underworld.

the primal ocean, and was ruled by Ereshkigal, the Lady of the Great Place. Like Hades, the Sumerian realm of the dead was dark and dreary. Even Ereshkigal herself dined on dirt and muddy water. Her sexual appetites were insatiable, linking her in a negative way to the Great Mother.

Homer's underworld

Even more than the Mesopotamian peoples, the Greeks saw death as a dreadful event, and the realm of the dead as a place of sorrow. According to Homer, in the endless night of Hades, the sun never shone and the spirits were mere shadows. A few inhabitants, however, had special privileges. The blind seer Tiresias was granted the use of his mind by Persephone, the queen of the underworld, and could speak to questioners once he had been given some sacrificial blood to drink. Elpenor, the friend of the Greek hero Odysseus, died after he drunkenly fell off a roof. He, too, was allowed to speak because his body had not yet been cremated, but other spirits were sad, silent shadows that flitted across the murky landscape. The souls of the dead lived in a vague, dreamlike state, which was so dreary that the warrior Achilles said he would rather be a slave in the upper world than a king in Hades. Occasionally, residents of the underworld were visited by heroes who found hidden

Cerberus, the Hound of Hades

Cerberus, a terrifying three-headed dog with a snake's tail, guarded the entrance to Hades and prevented anyone from returning to the land of the living. He was the offspring of Typhon, a monster with a hundred snake heads, and Echidna, who was half woman and half snake. Other monstrous offspring of Typhon and Echidna included the many-headed Hydra and the Chimaera, who had the head of a lion, the body of a goat, and the tail of a snake.

For the last of his 12 Labors, the Greek hero Heracles had to bring Cerberus to the world of the living. Hades granted his permission, provided Heracles use no weapons. The hero subdued the animal using strength alone. According to Roman poet Ovid (43 BCE–17 CE), Cerberus foamed with rage when he was carried into the bright sunshine, and as his spittle touched the ground it turned into the poisonous aconite plant. In contrast, Orpheus's music calmed the dog, allowing the musician and his wife Eurydice to escape Hades— although for Eurydice the respite was all too brief.

Below: Cerberus *by English artist William Blake (1757–1827). Blake's painting is an interpretation of* The Divine Comedy *by Italian poet Dante (1265–1321), in which Cerberus guards the third circle of Hell—where gluttons are punished.*

entrances to Hades, usually in caves, gorges, or geothermal outlets that emitted steam and heat.

Homer described swarms of dead souls shrieking in terror, some of them enduring eternal torment for crimes they had committed while alive. As a punishment for killing his own son and serving him to the gods as a test of their wisdom, Tantalus spent eternity reaching hungrily for fruit on laden branches that swung away from his grasp. Another dead soul, Sisyphus, strained to push a giant rock up a hill, only to have it roll down again just as he succeeded in moving it to the top. This torment was due to Sisyphus's tattling to the river god Asopus that Zeus had abducted his daughter. Other mortals punished in Hades included Ixion, Peirithous, Tityus, and Ocnus. While extraordinary sinners suffered extraordinary pain, most souls remained in a lackluster, boring state, drifting over a boundless meadow filled with asphodel, the plant of Hades. They were possessed by the same passions and fears that drove the living, but the gods gave them neither punishment nor reward.

Later beliefs about the underworld

In his work the *Republic*, Greek philosopher Plato (c. 428–c. 348 BCE) told the myth of Er, who had a near-death experience and described the underworld. In this account, some of the dead entered through holes in the earth and others through holes in the sky. The first group described life after death as unhappy, while the second group rejoiced amid beauty and happiness. Those who had dishonored the gods or their parents could expect horrible retribution. They might be flayed and dragged to death, then hurled down to Tartarus, the deepest part of Hades. Doers of good deeds, on the other hand, were rewarded in equal proportion to their actions.

According to the Roman poet Virgil (70–19 BCE) in his epic the *Aeneid*, the fortunate souls were admitted to the elysian fields or Elysium. In some myths, paradise was located in the Isles of the Blessed, and inhabitants were able to enjoy the delights of wrestling on the grass and wandering in forest glades, whereas the wicked were suspended in fire or forever blown in howling winds. After a thousand years, the Blessed were called by the gods to the Lethe, where they were made to drink some of its water. In this way they forgot their past and took up another life on earth. These visions of the afterlife as a place of retribution and even reincarnation were far removed from the Hades that Homer described, which was egalitarian—since everyone went there—but depressingly dull.

The underworld in other cultures

Underworld visions from a variety of cultures indicate that human beings have expected to be held accountable for the choices they made during their earthly lives. Their societies generally held out the promise of reward for good behavior and punishment for evil. According to ancient beliefs in India, depending on their virtue or lack of it, dead souls were sent to paradise, a place of torment, or back to earth for another attempt at living a decent life. Yama, the god of death in Hindu mythology, bears close parallels to Hades. He was a son of Vivasvat, the sun. His sister, Yami, was his constant companion and ruled the females in the underworld. According to the sacred scriptures called the Vedas, Yama was the first man to die. Because of his cruel deeds as a warrior, molten copper was poured into his mouth three times a day, until he had done penance for his sins. He was said to inflict feeble old age on humans so that they would be less inclined to behave badly. In later times, Yama became a harsh, punishing figure, who carried a noose and had green-eyed dogs for companions, echoing Cerberus, the three-headed canine guardian of Hades. Dead souls crossed the Vaitarami River—just as the Greek dead crossed the Styx River—and entered the judgment hall. This concept of death reflected the three-fold hierarchical social order of Indo-European warrior tribes, in which a ruler exerted his power over the ruled.

The ancient Egyptian god of the underworld was Osiris. Like Hades, he had a beloved consort, Isis, and similarly did not punish the guilty himself, but had a flock of lesser deities to do this distasteful work. Following a mortal's death, Anubis, the jackal-headed god, weighed the heart, the memory, and thought. If Maat, goddess of truth, said the balance was equal, Thoth, the ibis-headed god, determined that the soul could go on to the realm of the dead. Those who failed the test were eaten by Am-mut, who had the head of a crocodile and a lion's mane. Just as Cerberus guarded Hades, so a similarly frightening animal guarded the entrance to the Egyptian underworld.

BARBARA GARDNER

Bibliography
Bulfinch, Thomas. *Bulfinch's Mythology.* New York: Modern Library, 1998.
Graves, Robert. *The Greek Myths.* New York: Penguin USA, 1993.
Homer, and Robert Fagles, trans. *The Iliad.* New York: Penguin USA, 2003.

SEE ALSO: Cronus; Death and the Afterlife; Demeter; Dionysus; Earth Mother; Egypt; Furies; Gaia; Hecate; Heracles; India; Osiris; Persephone; Sisyphus; Tantalus; Theseus; Zeus.

HAPI

Hapi was a personification of the Nile River, and thus a god of fertility. He was immensely important in the Egyptian pantheon because without the river the region would have been too arid for human settlement. Hapi was sometimes referred to as "lord of the fishes and birds of the marshes."

Life in ancient Egypt was centered on the Nile River, and the waterway was worshiped as a god. Hapi (also spelled Hapy and Hepy) is the Egyptian name for the Nile. The name *Nile* comes from the Greek *Neîlos*; its origin is unknown, but it may be related to Egyptian *nwy*, "water." In Greek mythology, Nile was an ancient Egyptian king who confined the river within channels and helped to fertilize the country. He was the father of Memphis, who married Epaphus, the son of Zeus and the cow-maiden Io. In the Predynastic Period (before c. 2925 BCE), the name Hapi referred to both the river and the god, but later the god was called Hapi, and the river became *iteru*, meaning "the river" or "the running one."

The Nile River flows north from deep within the African continent. Every summer, it is swollen by heavy tropical rains in the south, especially in Ethiopia, and bursts its banks in Egypt. When the waters recede, the banks of the river and the floodplain are covered with rich, fertile silt, in which the farmers plant their crops. The Egyptian economy has always depended heavily on the river.

Although Hapi was worshiped by everyone in Egypt, he had no temples dedicated to him. Instead he was represented in the temples of the other gods, usually as an androgynous figure—a fat man with female breasts. His skin was green or blue. He was often depicted holding a tray, on which were the lotus of Upper Egypt and the papyrus of Lower Egypt, or two vases for libations of water. Hapi, therefore, represents a united Egypt. The symbol of this union, the *sema-tawy*, is a double image of Hapi, one on each side of a throne, tying together a lotus and a

Above: Two figures of Hapi tying the Upper and Lower kingdoms of Egypt. This carving dates from c. 1304–1237 BCE.

papyrus. Hapi also appeared as a territorial marker, holding a tablet with the name and symbols of the nome, or province, of the god in whose temple he was placed. As a god of the sacred river, he wore a fisher's belt and a crown of aquatic flowers on his head, with an *utchat*, an "eye of Osiris," on his forehead; he sometimes held a plate of the fruits cultivated on the Nile's banks. Less commonly, Hapi was represented as a man with two goose heads looking in opposite directions.

Hapi's origins

The mystery that surrounded the origin of the Nile River was paralleled by the stories of Hapi's life. According to one myth, he was born in the underworld below the Aswan Falls, where the primeval waters of Nun (the water of chaos) flowed. As a result, he was particularly worshiped in

Other Gods Named Hapi

Hapi (Egyptian *hpy*) was also the name of one of the sons of the falcon god Horus. The sons represented the cardinal points of the compass and also played an important role in the ceremony of mummification. Their heads decorated the lids of canopic jars used to preserve the internal organs of the deceased. From left to right below they were Qebshenuef, a falcon, who preserved the intestines; Dwamutef, a jackal, who preserved the stomach; Imset, with a human head, who preserved the liver; and Hapi, a baboon, who preserved the lungs.

Hapi (Hepu) was also the name of Apis (Egyptian *hpw*), the sacred bull consecrated to Osiris. Only one real bull was considered to be the sacred Apis at a time. When it died a new Apis was transported to Memphis on a boat with a specially built golden cabin. The festival of the Apis bull lasted seven days, and the bull was often consulted as an oracle.

Below: These canopic jars bear the likenesses of the four sons of Horus. Hapi is the one on the right.

Swentet (Aswan). In another account, Hapi was said to have been born on Bigehin, an island in the Upper Nile, and dwelled in the caverns of the nearby falls, which were ruled by the creator god Khmun. Khmun allowed Hapi to flood every year, causing the annual inundation.

Hapi had two wives, both water goddesses. Mut, or Muit, meaning "water's flow," was similar to Nun. She represented humidity, which was the origin of the primeval universe, although she never attained great prominence. The other wife was Nekhbet, a vulture-goddess worshiped in Nekheb, the ancient provincial capital of Lower Egypt. Nekhbet was associated with both fertility and creation. She lived at the entrance to the abyss, at the place where Hapi was born and Khmun ruled.

Sometimes Hapi was merged with other gods representing fertility, such as Osiris, in whose mythical cycle Nekhbet was also involved. A version of Hapi was merged with Sobek, the crocodile-god, as well as with Khmun, Hapi's ruler, and with Nephri, the lord of grain. Later Hapi became linked with Osiris as the husband of Sothis, a manifestation of Isis who appeared as the star Sirius. The isle of Bigehin, where Hapi was born, was also the birthplace of Osiris. Hapi was one of the few gods not completely banished by the heretical pharaoh Akhenaton (ruled 1379–1362 BCE), who considered him to be an incarnation of the only true god Aten.

José Alfredo González Celdrán

Bibliography

Hobson, Christine. *The World of the Pharaohs.* New York: Thames and Hudson, 1990.

Wilkinson, Richard H. *The Complete Gods and Goddesses of Ancient Egypt.* New York: Thames and Hudson, 2003.

SEE ALSO: Egypt; Horus; Isis; Osiris.

HARPIES

In Greek myth, the Harpies (meaning "snatchers") were female monsters who caused mischief, tormented wrongdoers, and carried souls to the underworld. They were known for their hideous appearance and smell.

In the earliest accounts, the Harpies were not monstrous—they were simply spirits who represented windy or stormy weather, and they were depicted as beautiful young women with wings. Over time, however, they developed into terrifying beasts. They had long, fair hair and the faces and upper bodies of women, but the wings, tails, legs, and claws of birds of prey, with sharp talons made of metal. They were always ravenously hungry, and would steal food or even eat their victims before carrying away their souls. The Harpies were repulsive to look at, and they spread filth everywhere they went. They stank so much that whatever they touched gave off a terrible smell.

There are several different stories of how many Harpies there were and where they came from. According to the eighth-century-BCE Greek poet Hesiod, they were the daughters of Thaumas, who was a son of Gaia, the earth goddess. In Hesiod's account, the Harpies were the sisters of Iris, the personification of the rainbow and a messenger of the gods. Other sources mention that they were the daughters of Typhon, another of Gaia's sons, and Echidna, a monster who was half woman and half snake. Some stories say there were countless Harpies; in others there were between one and four of them. At least four of the Harpies had names: Celaeno, Aello, Ocypete, and Podarge.

Left: A Harpy standing between two sphinxes on a Corinthian amphora (c. 725–c. 600 BCE). Sphinxes were believed to have a woman's head and a lion's body.

The Harpies could be sent by the gods—especially Zeus, Hera, and Athena—to punish people, and they were sometimes referred to as "the hounds of Zeus," but they could also cause problems on their own by stealing, destroying property, causing storms, and kidnapping people.

The Harpies and Phineus

The most famous myth involving the Harpies is the tale of King Phineus. He was a king of Thrace, in northern Greece, who offended the gods. There are various accounts about what he did wrong, but in the best-known version he remarried after his wife died, and, in his desperation to please his new bride, allowed her to torture his children, who ended up being blinded. In another version Phineus was granted the gift of prophecy, but foretold the future so well that he infuriated the gods by revealing their plans.

As punishment, Phineus was himself blinded, and the gods also sent the Harpies to make his life a misery. The monsters constantly snatched his food from his hands or spoiled it with their foul stench, so Phineus could never get enough to eat and grew painfully thin. He was finally rescued when Jason and the Argonauts came past Thrace on their journey to fetch the Golden Fleece. Two of the Argonauts, Calais and Zetes, the brothers of Phineus's first wife, decided to help the king, and drove the Harpies away to the Strophades Islands. They were going to kill them, but the Harpies' sister, Iris, persuaded the Argonauts to spare them if they promised to keep away from Phineus. In some versions the Harpies then went to Crete; in others they stayed in the Strophades.

The Children of Podarge

Podarge, one of the Harpies, was the mother of Xanthus and Balius, the two magical horses that ran like the wind and pulled the chariot of the Greek hero Achilles during the Trojan War. The horses' father was Zephyrus, the West Wind. The gods gave Xanthus and Balius to the hero Peleus as a present on his marriage to the sea goddess Thetis—the horses then passed to the couple's son, Achilles, when he went to Troy.

Soon after the horses were born, Hera, the wife of Zeus, gave Xanthus the power of speech, and during the Trojan War he spoke to Achilles. He warned him that although he would survive a forthcoming battle, he would die soon afterward. The Furies, the spirits of vengeance, struck Xanthus dumb to punish him for what he had told Achilles. When Patroclus, Achilles' best friend, was killed at Troy, both Xanthus and Balius wept, and Zeus was sorry that he had allowed them to get involved in the fighting and violence of humans.

The Harpies and Aeneas

The Harpies also played a role in the story of Aeneas, survivor of the Trojan War and the son of Aphrodite, goddess of love. After Troy was destroyed, Aeneas wandered far and wide until, following a prophecy that he would establish a great city, he went to Italy and founded Rome.

During his journey, Aeneas sailed to the Strophades Islands, where the Harpies were living. He and his men slaughtered some wild goats and cattle for food. They made offerings to the gods before eating, but as they sat on the beach to enjoy their feast, the Harpies swooped down, snatched their food, and spread stinking filth and dirt all around. The sailors moved to another spot, but the Harpies found them and ruined their food again. Aeneas ordered his men to fight, but their blades could not harm the monsters. Celaeno, the leader of the Harpies, told the sailors that, although they would end up in Italy, they would suffer terrible hunger as a punishment for trying to kill her and her sisters, and would not be able to found a city until they were so hungry that they had eaten their tables.

In Italy, after landing at the mouth of the Tiber River, Aeneas and his men were so hungry that they ate the round bread platters on which they had been served a meal. They realized that these were the "tables" to which Celaeno had referred.

Left: The Argonauts Calais and Zetes rescue Phineus from the Harpies in this engraving by French artist Bernard Picart (1673–1733). The overturned amphora indicates the damage caused by the monsters.

Above: Aeneas and His Companions Fighting the Harpies *by French painter François Perrier (1594–1649). The mischief caused by the Harpies was a means for the Greeks to explain bad luck in their lives.*

Delivering justice; stealing souls

According to Roman poet Virgil (70–19 BCE), who recounted Aeneas's travels in the *Aeneid*, in her speech to Aeneas and his men, Celaeno refers to herself as "the eldest of the Furies." The Furies (or Erinyes) were the female spirits of justice and vengeance who punished wrongdoers, often by driving them insane. The myth of Pandareos also links the Harpies to the Furies. Pandareos was a man from Crete who upset Zeus by stealing his golden dog and giving it to Tantalus, one of Zeus's sons by the Titaness Pluto. Zeus turned Pandareos into stone as a punishment. His daughters, Clytia and Cameira, were cared for by Aphrodite, who fed them milk and honey and found husbands for them, but just as the two young women were about to be married, the Harpies took them away to be slaves to the Furies.

The Harpies' connections with the Furies, as well as their actions in other myths, suggest that people believed that they were able to carry away the souls of the dead. Female spirits or superhuman beings who had this power are found in stories from many ancient cultures. In Norse myth, the Valkyries took dead warriors into Valhalla, where they lived in a great hall alongside the chief god Odin. Like the Harpies, the Valkyries could be either beautiful or terrifying. In Egyptian myth, the goddess Taweret carried the dead into the next world, while the Celts believed that this role was performed by Morrigan, a raven-goddess who ate the flesh of dead people and carried away their souls.

The meaning of the Harpies

To the ancient Greeks, the Harpies represented the punishment that came from displeasing the gods, but they were also associated with unfairness and random bad luck. Like the winds that they originally embodied, the Harpies could come out of nowhere, ruin plans, and destroy people's lives. People blamed them for storms (see box, page 614) and for any small objects or items of food that mysteriously went missing.

In modern times, the word *harpy* is sometimes used to mean a mean, heartless woman. However, some people

Above: A terra-cotta Harpy overlooking the Aegean Sea on the Greek island of Thera. The Harpies were first known as weather spirits, and the Greeks often blamed them for causing storms.

Mythology and the Weather

The Harpies' names reflect the fact that they were originally storm spirits: *Celaeno* means "storm cloud," *Aello* means "rainstorm," *Ocypete* means "swift flier," and *Podarge* means "swift-foot." Although they developed into monstrous creatures, they continued to be associated with weather and were blamed for strong winds and storms.

Many gods, spirits, and monsters in mythologies from around the world are associated with different kinds of weather. In Greek mythology, for example, the Harpies' sister Iris was the goddess of the rainbow, and the god Aeolus controlled the winds. In Australian Aboriginal mythology, the Rainbow Serpent, one of the most powerful of all deities, controlled storms, rain, and floods. Many cultures have a god of rain, such as En-kai or Ngai, the rain god of the African Masai people. Since weather comes from the sky, it makes sense that people throughout history have interpreted rain, thunder, rainbows, and other forms of weather as signs, punishments, or rewards from the gods, who were usually thought to live above Earth.

also see the Harpies as a symbol of feminism, because they were strong female characters who represented male fears about female power.

Sources and cultural impact

A number of ancient authors gave accounts of the Harpies, including the Greeks Hesiod, Apollonius of Rhodes (third century BCE), and Apollodorus (second century BCE) and the Roman Virgil. In the *Odyssey*, Homer (ninth–eighth century BCE) describes the Harpies as wind spirits.

Many artists have depicted the Harpies. They appear in pictures on ancient Greek vases and temple carvings, and they have inspired more recent works, including paintings by French illustrator Gustav Doré (1832–1883) and British Pre-Raphaelite painter Evelyn de Morgan (c. 1850–1919).

ANNA CLAYBOURNE

Bibliography

Apollonius Rhodius, and R. C. Seaton, trans. *The Argonautica.* Boston, MA: Harvard University Press, 1990.

Rose, Carol. *Giants, Monsters, and Dragons.* New York: Norton, 2000.

Virgil, and Robert Fitzgerald, trans. *The Aeneid.* New York: Everyman's Library, 1992.

SEE ALSO: Achilles; Aeneas; Crete; Death and the Afterlife; Furies; Gaia; Jason; Natural Forces; Tantalus; Valkyries; Zeus.

HEBE

Hebe, meaning "bloom of youth," was worshiped by the Greeks as the goddess of youth. She was the daughter of Hera and Zeus, although one account suggests Hera became pregnant with Hebe after touching a lettuce.

After Hebe's birth, the gods competed to honor her with their gifts. Both Athena and Poseidon gave her intricate toys, while Apollo tried to surpass them by soothing Hebe with his music. Hebe grew into the form of a beautiful youth—Greek poet Pindar (c. 522–c. 438 BCE) described her as "fairest of all goddesses," and coins discovered near the Greek city of Argos depict her as a young woman in a sleeveless dress.

Cupbearer and wife

As a minor deity, Hebe performed tasks for the other gods. In his epic poem the *Iliad*, Greek writer Homer (ninth–eighth century BCE) describes how she prepared her mother Hera's chariot for battle, harnessing the horses and helping Hera into the chariot. Homer also relates how she looked after her brother, the war god Ares, when he was wounded during the Trojan War by Greek hero Diomedes. According to Homer, Hebe "washed him clean and put delicate clothing on him." Her most famous role, however, was as the gods' cupbearer, providing them with their favorite drink, nectar. She did not retain this role for long. According to one myth, Zeus gave her cupbearing duties to the handsome mortal Ganymede, with whom Zeus had fallen in love. He abducted the youth, installed him on Mount Olympus, and then made him immortal.

Another myth relates that Hebe stopped acting as cupbearer when she married Heracles, who achieved immortality after his death. Hera, who had previously hated Heracles, reconciled herself with the new god by adopting him and arranging his marriage to her daughter. Hebe bore Heracles two sons, Alexiares and Anicetus. It is possible

Right: The graceful figure of Hebe *(1796) was so popular that Italian sculptor Antonio Canova (1757–1822) carved four replicas of his original statue.*

Above: This fresco in the Corsini Villa, south of Florence, Italy, is by Giovanni de San Giovanni (1592–1633). It depicts Jupiter driving Hebe away in order to give her cupbearing duties to Ganymede.

that Hebe's change of status reflected the changing nature of ancient Greek society, which became increasingly patriarchal, or male dominated. An early name for Hebe was Ganymeda, which suggests that the concept of this deity split into two entities: the male, Ganymede, who took over the active role of cupbearer, and the female, Hebe, who adopted the more passive duties of a wife.

A different Hebe

Classical scholar Robert Graves (1895–1985) suggested that the deity who married Heracles might have been an entirely different Hebe from the Greek goddess of youth. He cited evidence from a collection of Greek songs addressed to the hero Orpheus, the Orphic Hymns, which were produced between the third century BCE and the fourth century CE. Two songs in this collection state that Heracles married a goddess called Hipta, whose many alternative names included Hebe. Hipta was worshiped as Mother Earth by the people of Mitanni, an empire in northern Mesopotamia (present-day Iraq) that flourished from approximately 1500 to 1360 BCE. This version of Hebe, known throughout the Middle East, might reflect Heracles' association with Anatolia (part of present-day Turkey), where, according to myth, he carried out 3 of his 12 famous labors.

Youth-giving qualities

As the personification of youth, the Greeks identified Hebe with qualities such as vigor, bravery, and generosity, as well as recklessness, arrogance, and inconsistency. In myths she had the power to restore people to their youth. The sorceress Medea made an altar to Hebe when turning the hero Jason's father, Aeson, into a young man again. Iolaus, Hercules' nephew and assistant on earth, prayed to be restored to his youth in order to kill Eurystheus, the king who had set Heracles his 12 tasks and mistreated both Iolus and his family. As Heracles' wife, Hebe readily granted Iolaus his request.

Hebe's two main centers of worship in ancient Greece were at Phlios and Sicyon, both cities on the Peloponnese peninsula that held allegiance to the region's chief city, Sparta. The Greek traveler and geographer Pausanias, who lived in the second century CE, wrote that one of the main things people requested from the goddess was forgiveness for wrongdoing. Released prisoners in Phlios honored Hebe by leaving their prison-chains on trees in a sacred grove.

ANDREW CAMPBELL

Bibliography
Bulfinch, Thomas. *Bulfinch's Mythology.* New York: Modern Library, 1998.
Graves, Robert. *The Greek Myths.* New York: Penguin USA, 1993.

SEE ALSO: Ares; Ganymede; Hera; Heracles; Jason; Medea; Orpheus; Zeus.

HECATE

The goddess Hecate, whose name means "she who works her will," occupies an ambiguous place in Greek mythology. In early accounts she is an all-powerful deity associated with brightness, yet later writers connected her with darkness and the underworld.

Above: A 16th-century Italian woodcut of the goddess Hecate from the book Mythologiae *by Natalis Comitis. Hecate is depicted with three animal heads, a variation on her more usual form of three bodies.*

According to eighth-century-BCE Greek poet Hesiod's epic account of the origins of the gods, *Theogony*, Hecate was a goddess who had strong links to the Titans, the divine race that flourished before the Olympian gods. Her mother was Asteria, the daughter of Titans Coeus and Phoebe; her father was Perses, the son of Titans Crius and Eurybia. In Hesiod's version, Hecate had a special status among the Titans and controlled the three earthly realms: the land, the sea, and the sky. Other divine beings sacrificed and prayed to her because she had the power to bestow wealth and blessing.

A new world order, however, commenced when Zeus vanquished his father, the Titan Cronus, in a ten-year-long battle that put an end to the reign of the Titans and ushered in the rule of the Olympians. Unlike the Titans, whom Zeus imprisoned in Tartarus, a terrible place far below the earth, Hecate was allowed to keep her honors and privileges. In addition, Zeus made her the benefactor of rulers, farmers, horse riders, and sailors, with the power to grant victory in battle and in athletic contests. He also named her the nurse of all the babies who survived to see their second day of life. Hecate reciprocated by fighting on the side of the gods in their epic battle against the Giants, during which she slayed the Giant Clytius with torches—objects with which she was often associated.

Downgrading a deity

In *Theogony*, Hecate's great powers and authority placed her above the Olympian goddesses who oversaw such areas of life as marriage, love, sex, and domestic affairs. However, in later centuries, Greek writers such as fifth-century-BCE dramatist Euripides and third-century-BCE poet Apollonius of Rhodes downgraded Hecate's imposing powers to put her on a par with other goddesses. They described Hecate as a goddess of sorcery and poisoning, whose presence preceded doom and destruction. One reason for this change may have been that, by the time of Greece's classical era (479–338 BCE), an all-powerful female deity did not suit the requirements of its patriarchal, society. The Greek pantheon reflected this male-centered society—the gods ruled the universe and the goddesses played subsidiary roles.

Hecate's treatment in mythology resembles that of another old and powerful female god, Gaia, the primordial goddess of the earth, who mated with Uranus to give birth

to the Titans. As happened with Hecate, Gaia's authority was subsumed by the Olympian gods, but she retained some prestige as a result of her earlier power. Both goddesses may represent the attempt to assimilate pre-Greek deities into the Greek pantheon. Gaia's origins can be traced back to the Pelasgians, Stone Age Greeks who strongly believed in a mother goddess. Some scholars think that Hecate may first have been worshiped by the Carians, an ancient people of western Asia.

Changing reputation

As well as downgrading Hecate's status from that described in *Theogony*, later writers further broke with Hesiod's account by associating the deity with darkness and destruction. One possible source for this change may be the "Homeric Hymn to Demeter," an anonymous poem—once thought to have been the work of the ninth- or eighth-century-BCE Greek poet Homer—written in or around the seventh century BCE. The poem tells the story of the abduction of Persephone by Hades, king of the underworld. Demeter, Persephone's mother and the

goddess of corn, does not know where her daughter has gone and despairs of finding the culprit. She is counseled by Hecate, whose "shining headband" and torch symbolize the light of understanding. Hecate tells Demeter that she has heard the voice of the abductor but has not seen his identity. She suggests that they seek out the sun god Helios, whose lofty position makes him privy to many secrets. Helios reveals that Hades is the perpetrator. After mother and daughter have been reunited, Hecate lovingly tends Persephone. Because Persephone is forced to spend part of every year with Hades, Hecate becomes her attendant in the underworld.

Two aspects of the poem may have influenced Hecate's later, sinister reputation. The first is that Hecate lives in a cave, a part of the earth that links what is above the ground to what is underneath it. Caves are also associated with monsters—in Homer's epic the *Odyssey*, the giant one-eyed Cyclopes live in caves. The second aspect is Hecate's role as Persephone's servant in the underworld. This role foreshadowed the deity's connections with death and dark forces. In his epic the *Aeneid*, Roman writer Virgil (70–19 BCE) describes Hecate as "queen of the sky and the dark domain below the earth," which emphasizes her estrangement from the world of mortals, who could not journey to either of these realms. Many Roman writers also identified her as one aspect of the triple moon-goddess, called Luna in heaven, Diana on earth, and Hecate below the ground.

Hecate's mythological transformation, from Hesiod's account to that of later writers, contains a series of reversals. Initially she was a goddess of light, but later her torches signified not their own light but the darkness that they dispelled. Hecate had also been a goddess of blessing, who was honored for making crops grow. According to later writers, however, her role was quite different: Hecate governed the harmful and destructive weeds that sprouted into the earth from the underworld.

Hecate's ambiguous role

In classical Greece and later, people believed that Hecate inhabited the space between the world of the dead and the world of the living. This position made her a frightening goddess, but also suggests an ambiguity—she may have been both bad and good. The idea that Hecate could cross normally unbridgeable boundaries shows up in the myths

that developed her darker side. She was the goddess of highways and especially of crossroads, where, according to Virgil, she could be invoked at night by cries of alarm. Travel in the ancient world was notoriously dangerous, and bandits often ambushed people at crossroads at nighttime. For some people, Hecate may have personified the evil forces operating at night and, in order to appease her, they left food offerings called "Hecate's supper" at crossroads. Other people, however, may have looked to the goddess to keep away evil spirits—pillars known as Hecateae were erected at crossroads and doorways for this purpose.

Magic, gods, and monsters

Hecate appears in many myths as a deity with magical powers, and one from whom mortals could learn dark secrets. In Virgil's *Aeneid*, the Sibyl, or prophetess, of Cumae orders Aeneas to sacrifice to Hecate upon entering the underworld. Then she guides Aeneas safely through this realm, because she has learned all about it from Hecate. In his account of Jason and the Argonauts, Apollonius of Rhodes tells how Hecate taught the witch Medea to use magic herbs. Roman poet Ovid (43 BCE–17 CE) elaborated that Hecate's followers picked their poisonous herbs in the dark of the moon. Worshipers used honey as a libation for the goddess, one of many traditional offerings to the dead.

Hecate was connected with many divinities and monsters. According to several sources, she mated with the sea god Phorcys and gave birth to Scylla, a beautiful nymph who, when she grew up, rejected all her suitors. The witch Circe grew jealous of Scylla's charms and poisoned the pool in which she swam, causing six terrible dogs to sprout from her body. Greek historian and geographer Pausanias (143–176 CE) mentions Hecate in his account of the Trojan War. When a lack of wind prevents the Greek forces from sailing to Troy, the seer Calchas declares that Agamemnon, king of Mycenae and commander of the Greek army, must sacrifice his daughter Iphigeneia to appease the goddess Artemis. In Pausanias's retelling, Iphigeneia does not die at her father's hand but, by the will of Artemis, becomes Hecate. This curious mythological variant can be explained by the association of Iphigeneia with Artemis, and of Artemis with Hecate. Many scholars consider Iphigeneia to have been a form of Artemis, while Hecate represented the dark side of Artemis. In her role as

Above: Hecate *by English artist and poet William Blake (1757–1827). The painting shows Hecate's three bodies and depicts the goddess surrounded by real and imaginary creatures in a nightmarish scene.*

the goddess of highways and meeting points, Hecate was sometimes known as Artemis of the Crossroads. Roman writers' identification of Hecate as one aspect of the moon, with Diana—the Roman name for Artemis—as another aspect, further strengthens the connection between the two deities.

Representations of Hecate

A number of surviving descriptions and representations of Hecate reveal her as having three complete bodies joined together. This form makes her slightly different from the mythical character Geryon, whose herds of cattle the hero Heracles stole as his 10th labor and who had three torsos joined at the waist. One explanation for Hecate's three bodies is her association with crossroads—three bodies would allow the goddess to look in all directions at once. Virgil called Hecate the triple-shaped Diana and the three-faced virgin—the latter description indicates that he did not credit her as the mother of Scylla. Pausanias, however, observed that in Hecate's temple on the Greek island of

Aegina the statue of the goddess had only one head and body. He believed that it was the fifth-century-BCE sculptor Alcamenes who originated her triple-bodied form in a statue that the Athenians called Epipurgidia, meaning "on the tower." Apollonius of Rhodes wrote that Hecate wore on her head a wreath of serpents entwined with oak leaves, a description that links her to the three female monsters known as the Gorgons. Hecate appears in the frieze on the Great Altar of Zeus (c. 180 BCE), which archaeologists discovered on the site of the ancient Greek city of Pergamum. The frieze depicts the battle between the Olympian gods and the Giants, in which Hecate fought on the side of the gods.

KATHRYN CHEW

Bibliography

Apollonius Rhodius, and R. C. Seaton, trans. *The Argonautica.* Boston, MA: Harvard University Press, 1990.

Hamilton, Edith. *Mythology.* Boston, MA: Black Bay Books, 1998.

Hesiod, and M. L. West, trans. *Theogony; and Works and Days.* New York: Oxford University Press, 1999.

SEE ALSO: Aeneas; Artemis; Circe; Cyclopes; Demeter; Diana; Gaia; Giants; Gorgons; Greece; Hades; Helios; Heracles; Iphigeneia; Jason; Medea; Persephone; Sibyl; Titans; Zeus.

HECTOR

Hector is one of the main characters in the stories of the Trojan War. A Trojan prince and elder brother of Paris, he was viewed even by his ancient Greek enemies as being noble, honest, and fearsome in battle.

Hector was the eldest of the many children of King Priam of Troy. Although it was another of Priam's sons, Paris, who triggered the Trojan War by running away with Helen, wife of Spartan king Menelaus, the ancient Greeks viewed Hector with respect and admiration. He was their enemy, but he was also a figure of great courage and principle. The Greeks also believed that there was ill feeling between the brothers and that Hector criticized Paris for abducting Helen, even though his loyalty to his brother and his city then led him to fight for Paris's cause.

During the Trojan War, Hector was the leader of the Trojan forces in their battle against the besieging Greeks. Yet Hector's story is more than simply a tale of military might; it also emphasizes the importance the ancient Greeks placed on the institution of the family. In Homer's *Iliad*, thought to date from around 800 BCE, there is one emotional scene in particular when Hector, fresh from his feats on the battlefield, enjoys a happy moment with his wife, Andromache, and their young

Right: This is a model for the statue of Hector created by Italian sculptor Antonio Canova (1757–1822).

son, Astyanax. Later in the story Homer also tells of the deep grief felt by Andromache and the Trojans in general at the news of Hector's death.

Greece, Troy, and the Trojan War

The ancient city of Troy was part of the network of city-states around the Mediterranean with which Greece traded and interacted. According to legend, King Priam was a descendant of Zeus. A seer told him that the newborn Paris would one day bring destruction to Troy, so Priam abandoned the baby on a mountainside to die, but he was soon rescued by a shepherd. When he grew up, Paris returned to Troy. Priam then sent him to Greece, where he visited King Menelaus of Sparta. Aphrodite, goddess of love, had promised Paris that he would marry the most beautiful woman in the world, who was Menelaus's wife, Helen. Helen and Paris ran away together and settled in Troy. When the Greeks learned of this affront to the king, they assembled an army and sailed to Troy to attack the city and win back Helen. This began the Trojan War.

King Priam was very old when the war began, so his son Hector was chosen as leader of the Trojan army. Hector was the obvious choice as leader not just because he was the prince but because he was renowned for his military skill. The Greeks knew that unless they could kill him, they would probably fail to topple Troy. Hector was a formidable enemy, and he was often helped by the god Apollo (see box, page 622). This was partly why, according to legend, the Trojan War lasted for as long as 10 years.

Above: This painting by Giovanni Demin (1786–1859) depicts Hector, on the right wearing a large helmet, urging his brother Paris, in the center almost nude, to do the noble thing and join in the fight against the besieging Greeks. Helen, wearing a white dress, sits on Paris's right. The scene takes place in a temple dedicated to Aphrodite.

Even though Hector was a skilled warrior and killed many of the Greeks' best fighters, such as Epigeus and Archesilaus, he did not enjoy war but rather saw the defense of the city as his duty. On one occasion he tried to resolve the war by arranging a duel between Paris and Menelaus, but Aphrodite interfered on Paris's behalf and the duel did not have a conclusive outcome.

The death of Hector

The Greeks' best soldier in the Trojan War was Achilles. However, after a disagreement with Agamemnon, the leader of the Greek armies, Achilles refused to fight, and the Trojans gained the upper hand. At this point Achilles' best friend and companion, Patroclus, decided to go into battle in Achilles' chariot, wearing Achilles' armor. He reasoned that if the Greek soldiers thought he was Achilles, they would be encouraged to fight harder. He was right, and the Greeks began to force the Trojans back toward the city. Seeing what he thought was Achilles joining the battle,

Intervention of Apollo

The Trojan War split the loyalties of the Olympian deities, with some favoring the Greeks and some the Trojans. One of the most powerful gods to intervene in the mortal conflict was Apollo. According to Homer, Apollo's involvement in the war came late, some nine years after the fighting began, when the daughter of one of Apollo's priests was abducted by Agamemnon. The angry god sent a pestilence into the Greek camp, ailing and killing many soldiers. Several of his later involvements directly involved Hector. When Hector was badly wounded by a large bolder thrown at him by the Greek warrior Ajax, Apollo was ordered by Zeus to heal Hector's wounds. Another more famous incident occurred when Patroclus was battling Hector. Apollo first knocked off Patroclus's helmet, then his shield and breastplate, and finally the deity split Patroclus's spear, leaving the Greek hero completely defenseless against Hector. When Achilles avenged his friend's death, Apollo was unable to save Hector from Achilles' deadly spear. Yet Apollo did preserve the Trojan's body while Achilles dragged it behind his chariot. Apollo also played a part in the death of Achilles. Before Troy fell, Paris shot an arrow at Achilles and Apollo guided the arrow toward the only vulnerable part of Achilles' body, his heel.

Hector was afraid. He knew that Achilles was the only fighter who could match him. Overcoming his fear, Hector fought his enemy in single combat, and since it turned out to be Patroclus and not Achilles, Hector killed him easily. Hector took Achilles' armor from Patroclus's body and afterward wore it himself.

When he realized that Hector had killed his friend Patroclus, the grieving Achilles resolved to take his revenge and rejoined the battle. Seeing the danger from Achilles, Priam ordered the Trojan army to retreat back into the city, but Hector refused. He stayed outside to fight Achilles, but then lost his nerve and began to run away. Achilles chased him around the battlefield, until the goddess of war, Athena, who favored the Greeks, deceived Hector. She appeared to him in the form of one of his brothers, Deiphobus, and encouraged him to stand and fight. Tricked into thinking he had his brother to help him, Hector turned to face Achilles. It was then that Achilles killed Hector with a spear wound to the neck.

After Hector's death

Not content with having killed Hector, Achilles strung the Trojan's body to his chariot and dragged it around the battlefield before taking it back to his camp. Urged on by Zeus, Hector's brokenhearted father, Priam, visited Achilles and begged to be given the body. Achilles took pity on the old king and released the corpse. Priam then returned to Troy with Hector's body and prepared it for a funeral.

Not long after Hector's death, the Greeks finally tricked their way into Troy using the Trojan Horse, burned most of the city to the ground, and took Helen back to Greece. Hector's son, Astyanax, was thrown from the battlements and killed in case he tried to take revenge after he grew up, and Andromache was taken prisoner.

Hector and Troy

In the story of the Trojan War, especially in Homer's version, Hector is not only a great hero, but also acts as a symbol of Troy and its fate. Like Troy, he is strong, solid, and unyielding and stands firm against the Greek attack for a huge length of time. Troy's hopes depend on him, and while he holds out, so does the city. Yet just as Hector is

Below: This sarcophagus depicts Achilles on his chariot dragging the dead body of Hector in front of the Trojans. Achilles finally released the body to the dead hero's grieving father, King Priam, for burial.

Hector as Cult Hero

In ancient Greece from about the third to the eighth century BCE, many legendary heroes, such as Hector, Heracles, and Achilles, had cult followings that rivaled the worship of the major Olympians. Generally such heroes were considered semidivine: for example, Hector's father, Priam, was said to have been the grandson of a river god; Heracles was the son of Zeus; and Achilles the son of the sea goddess Thetis. The tradition of worshiping a particular hero is known as a hero cult, and the followers of a particular hero cult would make offerings to their hero. For instance, they would sacrifice animals, such as sheep, or pour a liquid, such as blood, wine, or oil, onto the ground at the site where the hero was believed to have been buried. They would also pray to their hero to help them, and they believed that the hero would occasionally come back to life at the spot where his body was buried.

The cult of Hector was followed mostly in and around Troy, where he was thought to have been buried. There was also a cult dedicated to Hector at the Greek city of Thebes. This was because, according to one version of the legend, Hector's body had been removed from Troy and buried there.

Opposite: Tears of Andromache, *by French artist Jacques-Louis David (1748–1825), depicts the widow and her son grieving beside Hector's corpse. David chose to paint Hector because his qualities made him a popular hero during the French Revolution.*

doomed, so too is Troy doomed. The way Hector is tricked just before his death, and the humiliating way Achilles treats his body, are soon echoed by the Greeks. They trick the Trojans with the hollow wooden horse, and then burn and destroy the city and humiliate its people. Troy's weakness, like Hector's, is its refusal to do anything but keep fighting. Instead of negotiating or striking a deal that might end the war, Troy relies solely on its military power—just as Hector relies on his strength—and is taken advantage of by the cunning superiority of the Greeks.

Admiration of the Greeks

Even though Hector was a Trojan, the ancient Greeks respected him and regarded him as a military leader worth emulating. They admired his calmness, courage, and sense of duty, believing that these qualities were more useful on the battlefield than the unpredictable, often childish moods of his Greek counterpart, Achilles.

Hector never lied, cheated, or resorted to underhand tricks to win his victories (although Apollo did unfairly intervene on his behalf). He was always honest and honorable, the only lapse being when he took Achilles' armor from the corpse of Patroclus and wore it himself. He could not understand how others, such as his brother Paris, could be immoral, lazy, or ungentlemanly. In addition to lauding him in epic poems and myths, the ancient Greeks also depicted Hector in their art, and some groups even worshiped him like a god (see box, left).

Despite all of Hector's positive qualities, he was nevertheless a tragic figure. By linking Hector so closely to his family and by showing the emotional devastation felt by his wife at the news of his death, Homer demonstrates that the victims of war are not just the soldiers but their families as well.

Various sources of Hector

Homer's *Iliad* is considered to be the first major work about the Trojan War. A significant portion of the epic poem focuses on Hector's life during the final stages of the war, and the poem ends with his funeral. The *Iliad* does not include the fall of Troy, although Homer does mention this in his other great work, the *Odyssey*. A later dramatist, Euripides (c. 486–c. 406 BCE), featured Hector's wife, Andromache, in his play *The Trojan Women*, about the fate of the women of Troy after the city's defeat. Other classical writers, such as Pindar (c. 522–c. 438 BCE), Apollodorus (third century BCE), and Ovid (43 BCE–17 CE), reworked and added to the story of the Trojan War. It is from them that most of the details about the end of the war and the fate of Hector's family have been passed down.

Although in modern terms, Hector is not as famous as some of the other Trojan War characters, such as Helen, he has featured in numerous paintings that depict scenes from the Trojan War. He also often appears in works of literature regarding the Trojan War, such as William Shakespeare's play *Troilus and Cressida* and an opera, *King Priam*, by British composer Michael Tippett (1905–1998).

ANNA CLAYBOURNE

Bibliography

Euripides, and Nicholas Rudall, trans. *The Trojan Women.* Chicago: Ivan R. Dee, Inc., 1999.

Homer, and Robert Fagles, trans. *The Iliad.* New York: Penguin USA, 2003.

Shakespeare, William. *The History of Troilus and Cressida.* New York: Penguin USA, 2000.

SEE ALSO: Achilles; Apollo; Athena; Demigods and Heroes; Greece; Hecuba; Helen; Patroclus; Priam.

HECUBA

Hecuba was the chief wife of Priam, king of Troy, and the mother of many of his children, including sons Hector, Paris, and Troilus and daughters Cassandra, Creusa, and Polyxena.

There is no historical evidence that Hecuba ever existed, but she plays a major role in ancient Greek mythology. Ancient sources are divided on the names of Hecuba's parents. Homer, a Greek epic poet of about the eighth century BCE, described her as the daughter of Dymas, a native of Phrygia in western Asia, but according to Greek tragic playwright Euripides (c. 486–c. 406 BCE), her father was Cisseus. Other early writers give her mother's name as Evagora, Glaucippe, or Teleclia. However, Hecuba's importance in myth does not derive from her ancestry, but from her role as the wife of Priam and mother of several of his daughters and 19 of his sons, including Hector, the greatest warrior of the Trojans.

During Priam's reign, Troy was besieged for 10 years by the Greeks. According to Homer, the conflict ended when the Greek armies captured Troy, burned it to the ground, and killed or enslaved its inhabitants. All the stories about Hecuba are set against the background of the destruction of her city.

The fall of Troy

Until the war, Troy had been the wealthiest and most powerful city in Asia Minor. As Priam's chief wife and the mother of many of his children, most of them sons, Hecuba's status and happiness seemed assured. Yet the decade of the Trojan War stripped her of everything: her family, her home, her social status, and her personal freedom. During the conflict she sent her youngest son, Polydorus, to Polymestor, king of Thrace, for safety. When Troy fell to the Greeks, Hecuba was handed over to Odysseus as a slave. While accompanying Odysseus on his homeward journey to Greece, she discovered the corpse of Polydorus and avenged his murder by Polymestor by killing two of the latter's children and tearing out his eyes. Hecuba was eventually turned into a fiery-eyed dog.

Left: The Dream of Hecuba *is one of the panels in Pippi de' Gianuzzi's* Scenes from the Trojan War *fresco, painted in the late 1530s.*

Those are the bare bones of the legend of Hecuba. The story became popular with later writers, who did much to embellish her biography and character. Some of the details they appended are contradictory, however.

According to most Greek sources, the Trojan War began after the Trojan prince Paris, Hecuba's second son by Priam, eloped with the wife of Menelaus, king of Sparta. In response to this outrage, the Greeks mounted an expedition to rescue Helen from the enemy. According to Pindar (c. 522–c. 438 BCE), a poet from the city of Thebes in Boeotia (northwestern Greece), while Hecuba was pregnant with Paris she had a vivid dream that the son born to her was a firebrand that set fire to the city. The soothsayer Cassandra interpreted the dream to mean that Paris would bring destruction to the whole state. (In Homer's *Iliad*, Cassandra had been merely a daughter of Hecuba and Priam; her role as a prophetess was added by later authors.) Alarmed by this prophecy, King Priam gave orders that his child be left out to die on Mount Ida. Paris was rescued by a shepherd, however, and as a young man he was accepted back into the city, where he inevitably came to fulfill the seer's prediction.

All but one of Hecuba's children died during the Trojan War. Of the sons whose names were recorded by the author Apollodorus (fl. 140 BCE), a collector and probably an embellisher of myths, Antiphus, Deiphobus, Hector, Hipponous, Pammon, Polites, Troilus, and Paris himself were killed in combat. Polydorus, her youngest son, and her infant grandchild Astyanax (the only son of Hector) were murdered shortly after the end of the war. Her daughters Cassandra, Creusa, Laodice, and Polyxena all died during the fall of the city or shortly afterward. Hecuba's sole surviving offspring was Helenus, who spent some time after the war as a slave but later became king of Epirus.

After the war

In the *Iliad*—Homer's account of the ninth year of the Trojan war—Hecuba remains always in the background, fulfilling the role of the bereaved queen destined to survive the sack of Troy, the loss of her husband, and nearly all her children. The latter part of her life became a favorite subject of Greek tragedy. Hecuba features in two great plays by Euripides. In *The Trojan Women*, she is handed over to Odysseus at the end of the conflict and has to endure the sacrifice of her daughter Polyxena on Achilles' tomb and the murder of her grandchild, Hector's only son, Astyanax. Hecuba is powerless to intervene as her daughter Cassandra is given as a slave to Agamemnon, the leader of the Greeks, and as Andromache, her daughter-in-law, the widow of Hector, is handed over to another Greek captain. Finally Hecuba herself is led away, lamenting the fate of her city, as the slave of the Greek Odysseus.

Below: In this painting by Vincenzo Camuccini (1771–1844), Hecuba leaves her infant son Paris with shepherds. In other versions of the myth, the child was abandoned and found by shepherds on a mountainside.

In *Hecuba* Euripides gives a different account of the end of the queen's life. She discovers the murder of her last remaining son, Polydorus, and the prophecy is made that she will later be transformed into a dog. Her daughter, Polyxena, accompanies Hecuba on Odysseus's ship, but the Greeks then decide to sacrifice her to Achilles. Shortly after Polyxena's death, word is brought to Hecuba that the body of her son, Polydorus, has been found washed up on shore. As in other versions of the story, Polydorus had been sent for safekeeping to Polymestor, king of Thrace, at the beginning of the war, only to be murdered by the monarch once Troy fell.

According to Euripides, Hecuba exacted a savage vengeance on Polymestor. She went to Thrace, pitched camp, and enticed him and his sons into a tent, where she and other Trojan women murdered the king's own children before his eyes, and then blinded him.

Having lost everything else, Hecuba now lost her mind, and at last even her humanity. Euripides depicts her being driven mad with grief. In the end the prophecy was fulfilled: Hecuba was transformed into a barking dog; she threw herself from Odysseus's ship and drowned in the sea.

Hecuba in art

Although many of the great characters and exciting incidents from the Trojan War are frequently represented in art, there are relatively few paintings of Hecuba. However, there are two outstanding exceptions to this general rule. Italian Renaissance artist Giuseppe Maria Crespi (1665–1747)—known as lo Spagnolo—painted *Hecuba Blinding Polymnestor*, a masterpiece which is now housed in the Musée des Beaux Arts in Brussels, Belgium. Another famous depiction of the Trojan queen appears in the series of frescoes known as *Scenes from the Trojan War*. These were painted by Pippi de' Gianuzzi (c. 1499–1546) on the walls of the Reggia di Gonzaga (the ducal apartments) in Mantua, Italy.

LAUREL BOWMAN

Bibliography

Homer, and Robert Fagles, trans. *The Iliad*. New York: Penguin USA, 2003.
Homer, and Robert Fagles, trans. *The Odyssey*. New York: Penguin USA, 1999.

SEE ALSO: Cassandra; Hector; Helen; Odysseus; Paris; Priam.

HEIMDALL

The Norse god Heimdall was the guardian of Bifröst, a rainbow bridge that linked Asgard, home of the gods, to Midgard, dwelling place of mortals and giants. Only gods were allowed to cross Bifröst; mortals and giants were strictly forbidden even to set foot on it. Heimdall's other role was to blow a curved ram's horn to warn all the gods that the giants were attacking Asgard, signaling the start of Ragnarok, the end of the world of giants and gods.

Heimdall was one of the elder members of the Aesir, the Norse gods who lived in the mythical world of Asgard. Knowledge of Heimdall is scarce because only fragments of information remain concerning the legends in which he would have featured. The main source on Heimdall is the writings of Snorri Sturluson (1179–1241), an Icelandic historian whose most influential works include the *Prose Edda*, a treatise that recounts the myth tales in Icelandic poetry, and the *Heimskringla*, an extensive history of Norway. Yet by the time Snorri collated the Norse myths, many ancient legends, such as those pertaining to Heimdall, had either been forgotten or were only hinted at in a few lines of text or in names of characters. For example, Heimdall was sometimes referred to as Gullintanni, meaning "golden teeth," and he rode a horse

Below: This early-20th-century painting depicts Bifröst, the rainbow bridge that linked the world of humans to the world of the gods.

Above: This illustration from an early-18th-century manuscript depicts Heimdall blowing Gjallarhorn to signal the start of Ragnarok. According to legend, the noise from the horn would be so loud that all the creatures in the universe would hear it.

named Gulltopp ("golden top"), but no one knows why. In addition to Snorri Sturluson, other sources containing references to Heimdall include the *Völuspá*, the *Rígsthula*, and the *Hyndluljód*. All three were poems of Norse myths written anonymously: the first two served as sources for Snorri Sturluson, and the last appeared in the 14th century.

Heimdall's most important role was as the watchman of Himinbjörg, a kind of gatehouse or entrance to Asgard. Himinbjörg was Heimdall's home and was approached from Midgard, the world of humans, via Bifröst, a brightly colored bridge made from a rainbow. Bifröst linked Midgard to Asgard, and only the Aesir were allowed to cross it; humans and giants were strictly forbidden. The giants lived in a third world called Jotunheim, although many sources say this was a region of Midgard.

Heimdall made the perfect watchman. He had remarkable vision and hearing. He could see a hundred miles in all directions, day or night, and his hearing was so acute that he could hear grass growing in meadows and wool growing on sheep. He also required very little sleep. These talents proved useful because Heimdall's ultimate task was to sound a horn named Gjallarhorn (see box, page 632) when he spied the giants of Jotunheim amassing for their final attack on Asgard, an event known as Ragnarok.

Birth of Heimdall

According to *Rígsthula*, Heimdall also played an important role in the emergence of the human race. In this story Heimdall assumed the name Rig at the beginning of the world. *Rígsthula* in part is the story of Rig's travels. On his journey Rig stopped at the homes of three men—a noble, a farmer, and a slave. In each, he was welcomed and given a meal. He then spent the night in the bed of each host, lying between the host and the host's wife. Nine months later, the wife of each host gave birth. The child of the nobleman's wife was handsome and fair, the child of the farmer's wife was strong, and the child of the slave's wife was ugly. According to some scholars, the stereotypical difference in appearance of the three children is explained by Heimdall's adoption of the name Rig. *Rig* probably means "king" or "lord," and comes from the same Indo-European root that produced Latin *rex* and Sanskrit *raj*.

Other accounts of Heimdall's early life associate him with the sea. In *Hyndluljód* Heimdall was "imbued with the strength of … the chill-cold sea." He was also said to have been the son of nine sisters, each a giant wave, who were the daughters of Aegir, the Norse god (or giant) of the sea. Another of Heimdall's links to the sea comes from a version of his battle with Loki, the evil deity who led the

giants at Ragnarok. During their fight, Heimdall transformed himself into a seal.

Besides the sea references, Heimdall was also represented as a ram, when he was occasionally called Hallinskídi, meaning "asymmetrically horned," a name that may have arisen because of his Gjallarhorn. Several scholars have pointed out that in Welsh mythology the sea god Gwenhidwy is said to have given birth first to eight waves, called ewes, and then to a ninth and final wave, called ram. These same scholars suspect that, because of the sea and ram similarities between Heimdall and Gwenhidwy's offspring, there must have been a cultural and mythological influence from one group to another, but no ancient literary evidence supporting the theory has been found.

Odin's premonition

Ragnarok, meaning "twilight of the gods," would begin and end with Heimdall. According to Snorri Sturluson, who provided the most extensive account of the whole event, the blowing of Heimdall's horn would signal the start of Ragnarok. It would end when Heimdall and Loki, the last of the gods remaining, fought each other to the death. Ragnarok was to be an apocalyptic battle, and many ancient mythologies and belief systems around the world have similar stories that describe the end of the world.

The Norse god Odin, ruler of the Aesir, knew of the coming of Ragnarok long before it was to happen. Accounts claim that Odin gave one of his eyes in exchange for a drink from the well of wisdom, which belonged to Mímir, a giant. The well lay beneath the roots of Yggdrasil, the World Tree, which, according to some versions, was at the sacred center of the universe. As he sipped the water of wisdom, Odin saw a vision of Ragnarok. First he saw the many signs in nature foretelling the coming of the apocalyptic event. For example, animals gathered their food earlier than usual, and winter lasted for three long, cold years, or the "Fimbul Winter." Then earthquakes began as one of Loki's sons, the Midgard Serpent, wrapped himself around Midgard, shaking it until it cracked open. The seas then rose and flooded the land. Finally Loki himself, who had been chained up by the Aesir because he caused the murder of the beautiful god Balder, broke free and marched his other sons and the giants toward Asgard.

The twilight of the gods

When Odin's vision finally came true and the world had suffered the omens of the long winters, earthquakes, and the escape of Loki, all the enemies of the Aesir would unite to cross Bifröst. The rainbow bridge would collapse under

Heimdall's Gjallarhorn and Gabriel's Trumpet

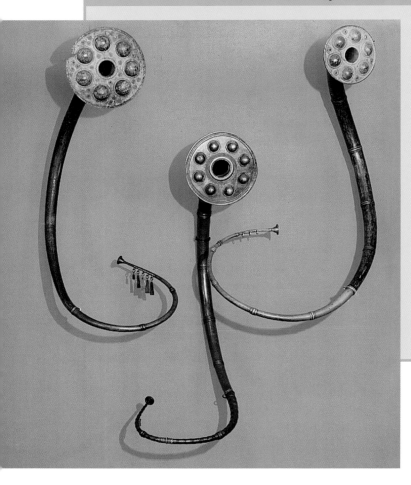

The final battle of the gods, Ragnarok, would begin when Heimdall sounded his horn to warn the gods of the approaching demons, giants, and monsters, enemies of the Aesir. The horn was first mentioned in the poem *Völuspá*, although it was not named. Thirteenth-century chronicler Snorri Sturluson expanded on this reference and named the horn Gjallarhorn, which may mean "the yelling horn." He described it as a drinking-horn and said it was the vessel from which Mímir, a wise being who was either a giant or a god, drank the water from his well of wisdom. The horn, according to Snorri Sturluson, was so loud that it could be heard everywhere, so that when Heimdall blew it, all the gods, humans, and other creatures would know that Ragnarok had begun.

In Christian mythology the archangel Gabriel is comparable to Heimdall in that he too blows his horn, a trumpet, to warn the world that Judgment Day, at the end of Armageddon, is beginning. It is believed that is when God will judge all Christians, living and dead.

Left: Three ancient musical instruments, called lurs, *from Denmark. Historians believe that such horns predate the Vikings.*

their weight, but they would still reach Asgard. It was then that Heimdall was to sound the Gjallarhorn to indicate that the battle was about to begin.

During the battle Thor, mightiest of the Aesir, would slay the Midgard Serpent, but as it was dying, the serpent would spit venom onto Thor, killing him too. Then the dwarves of the dark, enemies of the Aesir, would throw waves of fire on the earth, destroying all life, while the sun died and the stars fell from the sky. Odin would be devoured by Fenrir, a giant wolf who was one of Loki's sons. Then one of Odin's sons, Vídar—whom Snorri Sturluson compares to the hero Aeneas as depicted in the *Aeneid* by the Roman poet Virgil (70–19 BCE)—would kill Fenrir by stepping on the giant wolf's lower jaw and ripping its mouth apart.

As the battle raged, all creatures and things were to be destroyed, except for Heimdall and Loki, who would eventually kill each other, and the humans Líf and Leifthrasir, who would survive by hiding underneath Yggdrasil. As the world repaired itself, Líf and Leifthrasir would begin a new race of humans.

Echoes of Ragnarok

Parallel myths to Ragnarok exist in many cultures around the world, most notably in the Christian event known as Armageddon. According to Revelation, the last book of the Bible, Armageddon will be the final battle between the forces of good and evil, with the world ending in fire and the archangel Gabriel sounding his trumpet to herald Judgment Day (see box, above). Some scholars have suggested that Snorri Sturluson's version of Ragnarok was influenced by the sermons of Wulfstan, an 11th-century archbishop in England. Wulfstan's preachings were documented and had been made available in the 13th century, when Snorri Sturluson could have read them. Although the similarities between Wulfstan's Armageddon and Snorri Sturluson's Ragnarok are many, no direct link to the Bible or acknowledgment to Wulfstan from the Icelander have been found.

BARBARA GARDNER

Bibliography
Colum, Padraic. *Nordic Gods and Heroes.* New York: Dover Publications, 1996.
Orchard, Andy. *Cassell's Dictionary of Norse Myth and Legend.* New York: Cassell, 2002.

SEE ALSO: Apocalypse Myths; Balder; Creation Myths; Líf and Leifthrasir; Loki; Odin; Scandinavia; Thor.

HEL

Hel was the Norse goddess of death who ruled over Niflheim, the underworld. She was the daughter of the god Loki and a frost-giant, Angrboda. She had two brothers: Fenrir, a wolf, and Jörmungand, a monstrous serpent.

Above: This depiction of the Norse goddess Hel is by the German book illustrator Johannes Gehrts (1855–1921).

Hel was a terrifying goddess with a countenance that was hideous and threatening to behold. Her head and torso were living flesh, but her legs were rotting meat. She lived half in the world of the dead and half in the world of the living. In her great hall, Éljudnir, her table was Hunger, her knife Starvation, her bed Care, and her attendants Delay and Slowness.

Banishment

Hel did not always live in Niflheim. She had been cast into the outer darkness by the chief deity, Odin, in an effort to confound the prophecy of the Norns, or Fates, who had foretold that the children of Loki would destroy the Aesir, the main group of Norse gods. Odin treated Hel's two brothers with comparable severity. Fenrir—the name means "fen dweller"—was bound with Leyding, chains made of a magic metal. Jörmungand ("mighty wand") was hurled into the sea, where he wrapped his giant form around the whole earth—he was henceforth known as the Midgard Serpent.

Hel ruled over the nine lowest and darkest regions of the underworld, to which were sent all who died of illness or old age. Though originally known as Niflheim, her realm, and later the whole underworld, became increasingly referred to as Hel. This was partly after the goddess herself, and partly also because the name echoed—and was etymologically related to—the Christian hell. Christianity reached Scandinavia in the ninth century.

Odin's efforts to avert his fate would prove futile. The final outcome would be inevitably what the Norns had predicted. At Ragnarok, the final battle between the gods and the monsters, Jörmungand would be mortally wounded by Thor, but before the serpent died he would manage to bite his assailant, killing him with deadly poison. Fenrir would swallow Odin just before the wolf himself would be slain by his victim's son, Vídar.

Hel's revenge

After her banishment, Hel avenged herself on Odin. Loki had tricked one of Odin's sons, the blind Höd, into shooting another, Balder, with a dart of mistletoe. Balder died when the poison from the shrub entered his bloodstream. Odin then sent another of his sons, Hermód, down to the underworld to offer a ransom for the return of Balder. Hel refused, and Odin never recovered from the loss of his favorite child.

BARBARA GARDNER

Bibliography

Lindow, John. *Norse Mythology: A Guide to the Gods, Heroes, Rituals, and Beliefs.* New York: Oxford University Press, 2002.
Simek, Rudolf, and Angela Hall, trans. *A Dictionary of Northern Mythology.* Rochester, NY: Boydell and Brewer, 1993.

SEE ALSO: Balder; Dragons; India; Loki; Norns; Odin; Scandinavia.

HELEN

Helen, or Helene, was a mythic heroine in ancient Greece and a local divinity in Sparta. Reputed to have been the most beautiful woman of her time, and possibly of all time, Helen was the wife of Menelaus, king of Sparta, and the lover of Paris, a prince of Troy. Her abduction by Paris caused the Trojan War, and as a result she is almost always called Helen of Troy. Helen is the subject of several plays and poems, and according to one, at the time of her death she was made immortal by Zeus.

Helen's beauty is credited with causing the Trojan War—"the face that launch'd a thousand ships" according to playwright Christopher Marlowe (1564–1593). She was the daughter of the Greek queen Leda and either Zeus or Tyndareos, a mortal. The uncertainty surrounding the true identity of Helen's father lies in the myth of Zeus and Leda. Zeus fell in love with Leda, the wife of King Tyndareos, and transformed himself into a swan in order to mate with her. The children of this union were Helen and her brother, Pollux. On the same night Tyndareos made love to Leda and she became pregnant by him with Clytemnestra and Castor, who were mortal. The brothers became known as the Dioscuri, or "sons of Zeus." In antiquity, several places in Greece claimed to display the egg from which Helen was hatched.

Another older but less common version of the story has Nemesis, goddess of retribution, as Helen's mother, making Helen the daughter of two divine parents. In this version, in which Zeus was also said to have used the swan disguise, Helen was given to Leda to raise as her daughter. Nemesis was a divine personification of the punishment that awaits those who step out of bounds and commit the crime of *hybris* (exaggerated pride). The role of Nemesis as mother of Helen connects with a tradition that makes the Trojan War a form of divine retribution against mortals.

According to Stesichorus (fl. 600–550 BCE), a poet of ancient Greece, Helen's mortal father, Tyndareos, forgot to perform a sacrifice of thanks to the goddess Aphrodite during his wedding. Angry at the mortal's mistake, the goddess punished him by making his daughters faithless to their husbands: Helen was unfaithful to Menelaus and Clytemnestra murdered her husband, Agamemnon. Even as a young girl Helen's beauty made her vulnerable. In one myth she was carried off by Theseus, the Greek hero and slayer of the Minotaur, but was reclaimed by her brothers before any harm could come to her. Another similar version has it that as a result of her relationship with Theseus, Helen was the mother of Iphigeneia and entrusted the young girl to her sister, Clytemnestra, who was married and who raised the girl as her own. Most other accounts of Iphigeneia have Clytemnestra and Agamemnon as her real parents.

When Helen was a young woman, the news of her beauty spread throughout Greece, and as a result she had many suitors, especially from powerful, aristocratic families. Not wanting the young men's competition for Helen to cause strife, Tyndareos made her many suitors swear to support the claim of whomever Helen chose to marry and to avenge any attempts to take her from her legitimate spouse. In the end Helen married Menelaus, a son of Atreus of Argos, and they had a daughter, Hermione.

The abduction of Helen

Paris's seduction of Helen was the result of an incident known as the Judgment of Paris. Eris, the goddess of strife and discord, was angry at not having been invited to the wedding of Peleus and Thetis, so she disrupted the party by casting in the midst of the divine guests a golden apple, inscribed "To the Fairest." A dispute arose among the goddesses Hera, Athena, and Aphrodite over who deserved the honor, and Paris, prince of Troy, was chosen as the judge.

Right: This depiction of Helen, by German artist Franz von Stuck (1863–1928), was painted in the early 20th century. It shows Helen in classical pose surrounded by furniture and images of antiquity.

TADELT· NICHT· DIE· TROER· VND· HELLVMSCHIENTEN· ACHÆER,
DIE· VM· EIN· SOLCHES· WEIB· SO· LANG· AVSHARREN· IM· ELEND!
EINER· VNSTERBLICHEN· GŒTTIN· FVERWAHR· GLEICHT· JENE· VON· ANSEHN!

HOMER· ILIAS·

Right: The fourth-century-BCE sketchings on this bronze mirror depict Menelaus and Helen. The scene, one of the most popular in ancient Greek art, shows the moment when, after Troy has fallen, Helen reveals herself naked to her husband to stop him from killing her.

The three contestants were brought to the wilds of Mount Ida in Anatolia, where Paris, who lived as a shepherd, was tending his flocks. Each goddess offered a reward should he choose her. Hera offered rule over men; Athena, victory in battle; and Aphrodite, the most beautiful woman on earth. Paris gave the apple to Aphrodite, but soon discovered that his prize, Helen, was already married.

Intending to seduce Helen, Paris went as a guest to the house of Menelaus, where he succeeded in winning her over. Paris took Helen away, together with precious objects from the palace. This violation of hospitality angered the gods, particularly Zeus, protector of the relationship between host and guest, and Hera and Athena, who had a grudge against Paris because he chose Aphrodite over them.

The Trojan War

Menelaus and his brother, Agamemnon, called on all the suitors who had sworn the oath to Helen's father. They gathered a great fleet and sailed to Troy to reclaim her. Thus began the Trojan War, which, according to the poet Homer (c. ninth–eighth century BCE), lasted for more than 10 years.

Homer's *Iliad* is the most famous narrative of the war, and in it he portrays the relationship between Helen and Paris as less than harmonious. During the war she berates him for physical cowardice on the battlefield and resists his amorous approaches. She recalls the virtues of her previous husband and curses her own faithlessness, but after Aphrodite threatens her, Helen finally goes to Paris's bed.

Homer depicts Helen as a woman full of shame and at the mercy of desire. Although Helen was reviled by Priam's other sons, in Book Three of the *Iliad*, the old men of Troy see her and declared that there was no shame for the Greeks and Trojans in fighting over her beauty. Paris repeatedly refuses to give her up, and an attempt to settle the matter by a duel between him and Menelaus is deliberately sabotaged by Aphrodite.

After the war

The *Iliad* ends before the fall of Troy, so much of Helen's story comes to us from other sources. Late in the war, after Paris had been killed, Helen married another Trojan prince, Deiphobus. According to the poet Hesiod, who lived around 800 BCE, Helen and Deiphobus were the parents of a son, Nicostratus.

After the taking of Troy, Menelaus went in search of his wife with the intention of killing her for her faithlessness. In a scene frequently depicted on Greek vases, when he found Helen, she removed her robe and stood naked in front of him. He took one look at her beauty and the sword dropped from his hand.

The *Odyssey*, another epic poem attributed to Homer, gives a glimpse of the couple's home life back in Sparta in the years after the Trojan War. Helen is once again an obedient wife, but underlying tensions in her relationship with Menelaus are hinted at in a pair of stories that the couple tell separately to Telemachus, a guest who has come seeking news of his father Odysseus.

In Helen's story, she was loyal to the Greeks. For example, she says that she had recognized Odysseus when he disguised himself as a beggar to spy on Troy. When she realized it was the Greek king, she treated him well. Menelaus, on the other hand, answered with a story in which Helen teased the men inside the Trojan horse by

Below: The Love of Paris and Helen *by French artist Jacques-Louis David (1748–1825). As testament to the enduring popularity of the myth, this painting was made in 1788, over 2,500 years after Homer created his version of the story.*

Helen in Egypt

Egypt appears in several ways in Helen's story, not least in a version of the myth in which Helen never actually went to Troy. At the beginning of his *Histories*, Greek writer Herodotus (c. 484–425 BCE) traces the origins of hostility between Greece and Anatolia (Troy) to the stealing of Helen, and later tells of her stay in Egypt. In the *Odyssey* Homer says that, while attempting to return to Sparta, Menelaus and Helen are blown off course to Egypt, where they become guests of the king and are given many rich gifts.

In *Helen*, a play by Euripides (c. 486–c. 406 BCE), a phantom Helen goes to Troy while the woman herself stays in Egypt, where she is the guest of the king. The play begins as Menelaus arrives, conveniently at just the moment when Helen can no longer resist the king's demands to marry her. She meets Menelaus, who has been traveling with the phantom Helen, and confusion ensues. Once matters are cleared up, she tricks the king into letting her go back to Greece with Menelaus.

This alternate version of Helen's story dates back to a poem on the Trojan War by poet Stesichorus (fl. 600–550 BCE). In Stesichorus's poem Helen went willingly with Paris to Troy. According to legend, the poet was stricken with blindness as punishment for this slander against Helen. Stesichorus then wrote a palinode (recantation) in which he corrects himself and says that Helen actually never went to Troy. His revision worked and the poet recovered his sight.

using a divine talent she possessed to imitate the voices of their wives. She nearly induced them to betray themselves, but Odysseus prevented them by clamping a hand over their mouths. While each of these stories glorifies Odysseus in some way, they also reveal Helen's uncanny powers of recognition and imitation, as well as the difficulty of determining to whom she was loyal. In the same episode Helen eased the painful memories of all present by adding a drug to the wine. This drug, a gift from an Egyptian queen, called to mind a detour that Helen and Menelaus took on the way back from Troy (see box, above).

Throughout the *Odyssey*, as Odysseus struggles to return home and his wife, Penelope, resists the attentions of her many suitors, Helen and her sister, Clytemnestra, stand as cautionary figures for them both. In the underworld, Odysseus was warned by Agamemnon that he must return stealthily to his home on the island of Ithaca in case his wife turned out to be treacherous like Clytemnestra. Meanwhile Penelope strove to be a faithful wife in the face of great odds, and not a faithless one like Helen.

Helen as goddess

According to legend, both Helen and Menelaus were given divine honors after their deaths. Menelaus, although not a particularly highly regarded figure among Greek heroes, had an exalted position in the afterlife, apparently because he was the son-in-law of Zeus. He was said to have gone to the Isles of the Blessed, which were reserved for those of uncommon privilege. There was a shrine dedicated to him at Therapne near Sparta, known as the Menelaion. The couple was supposedly buried there, which suggests it was a hero shrine rather than the temple of a god. However, according to the fourth-century-BCE orator Isocrates, they were worshiped there not as heroes but as gods. One of the earliest inscriptions found in the region, a dedication inscribed on a sacrificial fork "to Helen," was found at this sanctuary.

The immortality of Helen is also suggested by Homer, who calls her "daughter of Zeus," a formula that he otherwise reserves for goddesses such as Athena. Some writers tell of Helen's posthumous marriage to Achilles on the island of Leuke, or White Island, in the Black Sea. Other suggestions of divine status for Helen come from the island of Rhodes, where she was supposed to have been hanged in revenge for the deaths of men in the Trojan War, and where there was a shrine to Helen of the Tree. Herodotus, a fifth-century-BCE Greek historian, tells the tale of an ugly baby girl in Sparta whose nurse brought her every day to pray in front of Helen's image at the Menelaion. One day a woman appeared, stroked the young girl's cheek, and predicted that she would grow up to be the most beautiful woman in Sparta. Indeed, so beautiful did she become that, like her patroness, she was also stolen from her first husband.

Helen as icon

Many other ancient Greek writers were fascinated with the figure of Helen. Sappho (fl. c. 610–c. 580 BCE), a female poet, wrote that the most beautiful thing is whatever one loves. She then used Helen as an example, not only of a desirable but also of a desiring woman, who followed "the thing she loves," leaving behind her husband and baby.

Just as Euripides' treatment of the phantom Helen (see box, above left) was influenced by contemporary philosophical thought about the nature of reality, orations by Isocrates in praise of Helen focused on the power of both eros (erotic love) and rhetorical persuasion. In this way, Helen, the most beautiful woman in the world, came to

Right: Helen on the Steps of Troy (c. 1870) by French artist Gustave Moreau (1826–1898). Moreau painted several versions of Helen, all of which depict her as the femme fatale who caused the destruction of Troy.

Homer and Helen

Although Homer reproaches Helen in his epic poem, he also associates her closely with epic poetry, which indicates his respect for her. When Helen appears for the first time in the *Iliad*, she is weaving a cloth showing the battles of the Greeks and Trojans—a type of textile counterpart to the poem itself, especially since ancient Greek poets are sometimes said to "weave" their poetry. In another scene, Helen stands on the wall of the city and identifies the Greek heroes for King Priam, providing the sort of heroic catalog that is typical of epic poetry. Only Achilles, of all the characters in the *Iliad*, is similarly associated with epic: when he has withdrawn from the battlefield, he sits alone and sings "the deeds of men." Helen, unique among Homer's characters, seems to understand the function of epic poetry and the meaning of mortal suffering. She tells her brother-in-law, Hector, that their sufferings are given by Zeus so that they will be the subject of song for generations to come. This is a succinct description of the function of Greek epic poetry, which is to provide lasting fame for heroic deeds.

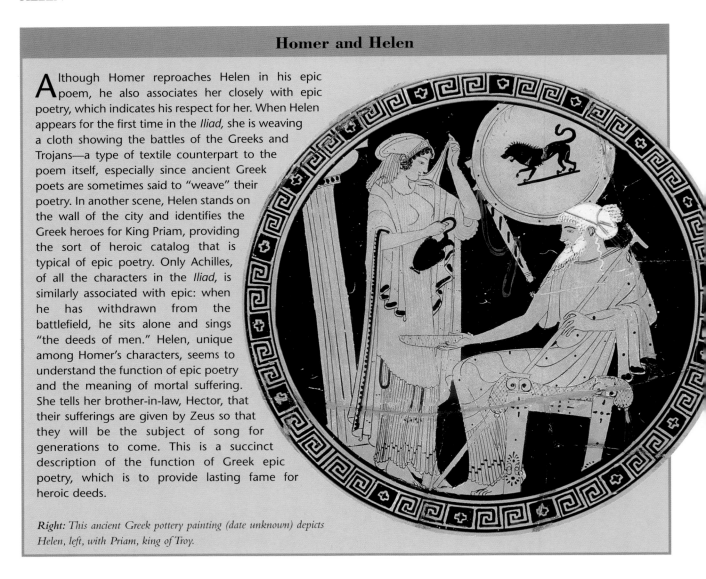

Right: This ancient Greek pottery painting (date unknown) depicts Helen, left, with Priam, king of Troy.

stand for any number of philosophical issues with which ancient Greek thinkers grappled. Helen is also an important figure in Euripides' dramas *The Trojan Women* and *Orestes*. In the former, she is reviled by all the captive women of Troy, while in the latter, Orestes and Pylades plot to kill her. Another classical writer who used Helen was the Roman poet Ovid (43 BCE–17 CE). He included a fictional letter from Helen to Paris in his work *Heroides*.

Helen has continued to play an important role in later Western literature. Medieval romances about Troy helped to keep Helen alive in the imagination. Edmund Spenser's *Faerie Queene* (1590) features a reworked version of Helen called "Hellenore." In the myth of Faust, as told first by the Elizabethan dramatist Christopher Marlowe and later by the German poet and playwright J. W. Goethe (1749–1832), the sight of Helen is one of the enticements with which Mephistopheles persuades Faust to sell his soul to the devil. Twentieth-century American poet H. D. (Hilda Doolittle, 1886–1961), frustrated with the male perspective on Helen, wrote from the point of view of the ancient Spartan beauty herself in her long poem "Helen in Egypt."

The fate of the Trojan Women and the story of Faust feature in operas including, among others, *Les Troyens* (The Trojans) and *The Damnation of Faust*, both by French composer Hector Berlioz (1803–1869), and *The Egyptian Helen*, by German composer Richard Strauss (1864–1949).

DEBORAH LYONS

Bibliography

Homer, and Robert Fagles, trans. *The Iliad and the Odyssey.* New York: Penguin USA, 1999.

McLaren, Clemence. *Inside the Walls of Troy.* New York: Atheneum, 1996.

SEE ALSO: Agamemnon; Aphrodite; Castor and Pollux; Clytemnestra; Greece; Hecuba; Iphigeneia; Menelaus; Nemesis; Odysseus; Paris; Theseus.

HELIOS

Helios, called Sol Invictus by the Romans, was the Greek god of the sun, but he was not one of the most important deities in the Greek pantheon. He was responsible for bringing light to the heavens and earth, usually by hitching the sun to his chariot and dragging it across the sky. As the sun god he could observe everything that occurred in the world during his daily journey from east to west. However, unlike most of the other Olympians, Helios had little interaction with mortals.

Helios, the sun god, was the cousin of Zeus, king of the Olympian deities. In Greek mythology they were both sons of Titans. The Titans were among the first offspring of the creation deities, Uranus (sky) and Gaia (earth). According to the *Theogony*, an epic poem of Greek mythology attributed to the poet Hesiod (fl. c. 800), two Titans, Theia and Hyperion, were the parents of Helios. Their other children were Selene (moon) and Eos (dawn). Two other Titans, Cronus and Rhea, parented most of the other Olympians, including Zeus.

In Greek and Roman art and literature, Helios is usually depicted as a youthful male deity with rays of light beaming from his head. He also usually drives a four-horse chariot. In some versions the sunlight emanates either from Helios's chariot or from Helios himself; in others the sun is attached to Helios's chariot and hauled across the sky.

Below: Helios in His Sun Wagon, *by Fabrizio Chiari (c. 1615–1695), is a fresco of the Greek sun god making his daily journey east to west across the sky, bringing light to to the world.*

Occasionally he is shown riding on horseback or having wings. The rays of light distinguish Helios from his sister Selene, whose head is often marked by a crescent moon. Helios, like Uranus, Oceanus (ocean), and Selene—all of whom embodied or were responsible for overseeing elements of nature—played a minor role in the stories concerning mortals and in the religious life of the ancient Greeks. In other ancient cultures, such as Egypt, the sun god had a much more prominent position; however, for the Greeks, Apollo, the god of light, emulated many of the characteristics of earlier sun gods (see box, page 643).

References to and children of Helios

It was generally believed that Helios rode his four-horse chariot across the sky from east to west each day, bringing light to the world. Each night he would sail in the celestial waters that surrounded the earth back to his home in the east in time to start his daily journey. Although there are few stories that feature Helios, he was said to have fathered several famous characters, such as Pasiphae, the mother of

Right: This Roman bronze head, from around the second century CE, is believed to depict Helios.

the Minotaur, and Aeetes, king of Colchis, father of Medea, and possessor of the Golden Fleece.

Another of Helios's sons was Phaethon, who pleaded with his father to allow him to drive the chariot for one day. Reluctantly Helios agreed, but the steeds proved too powerful for Phaethon to control, and the chariot scorched the earth. It would have destroyed all the mortals if Zeus had not intervened. The king of gods hurled one of his thunderbolts at Phaethon, killing him instantly. The youth's lifeless body fell from the chariot and landed in a river.

A few other stories either have references to Helios or include him in a minor role. For example, in the *Odyssey* Homer writes that Odysseus's companions slaughtered and ate some cattle that belonged to Helios. When the sun god learned of this, he traveled to Olympus and demanded that Zeus punish Odysseus's men. Zeus agreed and destroyed Odysseus's ship with a thunderbolt, drowning Odysseus's crew. Only Odysseus, who had not taken part in eating Helios's cattle, survived.

In another story, it is explained that Helios used a giant golden cup, forged for him by the god Hephaestus, in which the sun god and his horses rested as they floated around the earth each night, always reaching their starting point in the east in time to raise the sun again. Helios loaned the cup to Heracles when the hero was searching for the cattle of Geryon. The mythographer Apollodorus, who lived during the second century BCE, claimed that Heracles used his bow and arrow to force Helios to give up the goblet, which the hero used to sail far westward. On his return journey, Heracles again rode in Helios's golden cup and had room in the vessel for the cattle of Geryon.

Helios's Cult in Rhodes

The Greek island of Rhodes was the site of the main worship of Helios. It was believed that when Zeus originally divided the world among the gods, Helios was away in his chariot. Some time later, when Rhodes appeared, Helios claimed the island. In recognition of their patron, the people of Rhodes held an annual festival, the Halieia, where four horses were thrown into the sea to relieve Helios's tired ones. Also the Rhodians built the Colossus of Rhodes, a huge statue of Helios and one of the so-called Seven Wonders of the World. It stood at the entrance to the main harbor and served as a kind of lighthouse. According to legend, a nymph of the island gave birth to seven of Helios's sons, and three of his grandsons were the namesakes of three Rhodian cities: Cameiros, Ialysos, and Lindos.

Helios and Apollo

The ancient Greeks sometimes called Helios Phoebus, meaning "shining." Beginning around the fifth century BCE, Apollo, the Olympian god of prophecy and divination, was also called Phoebus. From then on Helios and Apollo were often identified with each other. Greek dramatist Euripides (c. 486–c. 406 BCE) wrote a short play *Phaethon* that made the connection between Apollo and Helios explicit for the first time in Greek literature. Scholars believe that Apollo, whom the Greeks believed was a son of Zeus and Leto, may have originated as a divinity in Asia and was adopted by the Greeks early on. Unlike Helios, Apollo intervened in the lives of mortals and featured in several myths. In Greek art Apollo was often depicted in a manner similar to Helios: as a youthful figure with rays of light shining from him. He was also adopted by the Romans and highly revered by Emperor Augustus (63 BCE–14 CE).

Below: This Greek bowl depicts Helios in his horse-drawn chariot with rays of light emanating from his head. The god Apollo, who was also linked to the sun but held a more prominent position in the pantheon than Helios, was often depicted similarly in Greek art.

Another story involves Helios and Hephaestus. Because Helios traveled so high in the sky, he was able to witness everything that went on. One day he saw the goddess of love, Aphrodite, making love to Ares, the god of war. Aphrodite was married to Hephaestus, and Helios felt obliged to tell the god of metalworking what he had observed. After hearing of his wife's adultery, Hephaestus fashioned an invisible metal net and captured the lovers in Aphrodite's bed. Hephaestus hauled the lovers before the other Olympians, who howled with laughter.

In a subsequent story Aphrodite took her revenge on Helios. She made him fall in love with a girl named Leucothoe. The girl died either because as a mortal she could not bear Helios's power when they had sex, or because her father buried her alive when he found out that she had made love to a god.

Although Helios did not appear frequently in Greek myth or have much direct religious significance in Greek culture, he did play an important role in watching over oaths. Because he saw everything that went on during the day, Helios was sometimes called on to be a witness to oaths. His omniscience also made him privy to whether oaths were being kept or not.

Sun gods in other cultures

In other ancient polytheistic cultures the sun god usually held a prominent or chief position in the pantheon. For example, in Egyptian religion the sun god, Re, was the

Right: In this statue, Helios is given the face and hairstyle of Roman emperor Caracalla (188–217 CE). Helios was the favorite god of Caracalla's hero, Alexander the Great.

Sol Invictus

The Roman god Sol Invictus, whose name in Latin means "the invincible sun god," was based on the Greek sun god Helios and the god of prophecy, Apollo, who was linked to the sun. Generally, the older Roman pantheon that included Jupiter, Mars, Venus, and so on maintained prominence in Roman religion, but Sol Invictus became increasingly important in Roman religious and imperial life from the first century CE onward. There was even a temple dedicated to the deity in Circus Maximus, an important site in the city of Rome. From the first to the third century, the importance of sun worship grew until Sol became the chief object of imperial worship. Even the father of Constantine I, the first Christian emperor of Rome who ruled the empire from 306 until his death in 337, dutifully worshiped Sol Invictus.

creator and master of the world. Re's rising and setting symbolized the cycles of death and renewal prevalent in life. His center of worship was the city of Iunu, which the Greeks called Heliopolis or "city of the sun." Other sun gods included the Syrian sun god, El-Gabal, whose supreme position was alluded to in depictions of the deity standing alongside an eagle, the sign of celestial authority; and the Hindu god Surya, who has temples dedicated to him throughout India.

The Romans

As the Roman armies and their culture spread throughout the Mediterranean from the second century BCE, the Roman belief system began to incorporate other religions traditions. The worship of the sun was no exception, and the god Sol Invictus (Helios) became increasingly important (see box, above). Christianity displaced the worship of Sol Invictus in the fourth century CE, although the imagery of the sun with its blinding light and fire remains an important motif in Christian theology and art. The sun god maintained considerable influence in the Greco-Roman mind through Helios to Sol Invictus and beyond.

BRIAN SEILSTAD

Bibliography
Bulfinch, Thomas. *Bulfinch's Mythology*. New York: Modern Library, 1998.
Howatson, M. C., and Ian Chilvers. *Concise Oxford Companion to Classical Literature*. New York: Oxford University Press, 1993.

SEE ALSO: Apollo; Egypt; Eos; Frey; Hephaestus; Heracles; Icarus; Odysseus; Phaethon; Selene; Titans.

HEPHAESTUS

Hephaestus was the Greek god of fire and metalworking. He was one of the 12 major Olympian gods, but the only one to be lame. The other gods constantly ridiculed Hephaestus for his disability—as a result his actions were frequently motivated by his desire to punish those who mocked and abused him.

There are two versions of Hephaestus's birth and lameness. According to the Greek poet Homer (c. ninth–eighth century BCE), Hephaestus was born to Zeus and Hera. When he took his mother's side in an argument, Zeus knocked him off Mount Olympus. After falling through the air for a day, Hephaestus landed on the island of Lemnos, permanently injuring his leg. One of the peoples on the island, a mysterious group called the Sintians, nursed the fallen god back to health.

This version possibly reflects the ancient Greek view that Hephaestus's attachment to his mother was excessive and deserved to be punished. In elite society in Greece, boys were raised by their mothers until they were of school age, at which time they would leave behind the women's quarters and join the company of men. Hephaestus's punishment from Zeus may have been because he preferred the company of women to men. The suggestion that Hephaestus was insufficiently masculine is enhanced by his subsequent physical frailty and the teasing he received from his healthier siblings.

The other account of Hephaestus's origins comes from the Greek poet Hesiod (fl. 800 BCE). According to this source, Hera created Hephaestus on her own in retaliation for Zeus's creation of Athena, the goddess of war and handicrafts who emerged from the king of the gods' head, but when Hephaestus turned out to be lame, Hera rejected her son and threw him out of heaven. He fell into Oceanus (the sea) and was rescued by the sea nymphs Thetis and

Right:
A classical bronze statuette of Hephaestus, depicting him trailing his left leg. Hephaestus's disability led to his humiliation by other deities—itself a reflection of Greek attitudes toward physical handicap.

The Greeks and Disability

The reactions of Hera and her fellow deities toward Hephaestus's physical handicap reflected the ancient Greek attitude toward infirmity. They saw it as a sign of inferiority—mental as well as physical. In Homer's world, physical beauty always accompanied mental agility, while people with physical problems were regarded as slow-witted. Ironically, Hephaestus did not fit this model at all—as his skillful creations demonstrate—but he was treated as though he did. The fact that Hera's sole attempt to create life apart from her husband resulted in a flawed offspring suggests that the Greeks believed that the female creative potential was insufficient on its own to produce viable beings. Hephaestus always remained a second-class citizen on Mount Olympus. He was the only major deity who worked for a living—this perhaps represents the encroachment of a lower artisan class upon the ruling leisured class in Greek society.

Eurynome, who instructed him in the art of metalworking. To punish Hera for her ill treatment, Hephaestus designed for her an exquisite throne of gold. When she sat in it, the throne entrapped her in a fine mesh of chains. None of the other Olympians could free her or persuade Hephaestus to release his mother. Finally Dionysus, the god of wine, succeeded in getting Hephaestus drunk. Under the influence of alcohol, he agreed to return to Olympus and release his mother. Vase paintings show Dionysus either supporting a drunken Hephaestus on the walk up to Olympus or leading Hephaestus, who sat on a donkey. Hephaestus's return to Olympus remained a popular artistic topic, although this story did not survive in literature.

Special powers

Hera's casting of Hephaestus into the primal waters of Oceanus and his subsequent rescue symbolize a second birth. Like other mythical characters who passed through the portals of birth or death more than once—such as Orpheus, Heracles, Asclepius, Hippolytus, and Dionysus—Hephaestus emerged with a special power. In his case, it was the power to control and give life to metals, including gold, bronze, and silver.

There were three different accounts of where Hephaestus had his smithy, or workshop: on Mount Olympus itself, in the active volcano of Mount Etna on the Italian island of Sicily, or on Lemnos. According to Homer, Hephaestus made two golden robots to assist him. Roman poet Virgil (70–19 BCE) related that Hephaestus had his cavernous smithy in Mount Etna. In Virgil's account, Hephaestus was in charge of the one-eyed giants the Cyclopes, who forged Zeus's thunderbolts.

Helping gods and mortals

Hephaestus assisted various deities and mortals with his artistry and metalworking skills. During the Gigantomachy, the war between the Olympian gods and the Giants, he killed the giant Mimas with red-hot pellets of metal. He then designed and built palaces for all the Olympians, as well as for the mortals Aeetes and Oenopion. According to the second-century-BCE mythographer Apollodorus, Hephaestus constructed a mechanical bronze dog that Zeus gave to King Minos of Crete; a gold wedding necklace for Harmonia, the daughter of the war god Ares and the love goddess Aphrodite; and the bronze rattles that Heracles used to put the Stymphalian birds to flight during one of his 12 labors. He also purified Pelops, son of the king of Lydia, after his treacherous murder of the charioteer Myrtilus, who had helped Pelops win his bride.

Hephaestus's work did not end there. According to some myths, he assisted in Athena's birth by splitting open Zeus's head with his ax and releasing the fully grown goddess. When the Titan Prometheus challenged Zeus's supremacy by giving fire to mortals, Hephaestus riveted him to a cliff—said to be Mount Kazbek in the Caucasus—where he was tortured. Hephaestus also helped create the first woman, Pandora, whom Zeus offered as a gift to Prometheus's gullible brother, Epimetheus. Hephaestus designed and composed her body from clay, and the other gods endowed her with personal qualities. When Epimetheus accepted Pandora, he condemned humans to a life of suffering because she released sorrow and disease from the jar she brought with her.

Love and revenge

According to Hesiod, Hephaestus married Aglaea, the youngest of the goddesses known as the Graces. Other sources, however, name Aphrodite as his wife, but Aphrodite preferred Hephaestus's strong, virile brother Ares, and continued her love affair with the war god after her marriage to Hephaestus.

The sun god Helios, who saw all things and often played the role of informant in various myths, revealed to Hephaestus that his wife had been secretly sleeping with

Right: Vulcan Forging the Arms of Achilles *by Italian artist Giulio Romano (c. 1499–1546). Vulcan was the Roman god of elemental fire, later identified with Hephaestus. Both gods were patrons of metalworkers.*

Ares. As he had done with his mother, Hephaestus exacted his revenge by indirect methods rather than direct confrontation. He may also have realized that he would be no match for Ares if an aggressive approach ended in a brawl. Instead, Hephaestus fashioned a chain that was inescapably strong, but so fine that it was invisible to the eye. He made the chain into a net, fastened it over and around the marital bed, and loudly announced that he intended to visit Lemnos on business. As soon as they thought he had departed, Aphrodite and Ares climbed into bed, but found themselves caught fast in the invisible net. At this point Hephaestus returned, accompanied by the rest of the Olympian gods. His shame at having been cuckolded was tempered by the comedy in the couple's naked and public embarrassment. This story demonstrated to the ancient Greeks what happens when a weak male marries a strong female: the husband is disgraced by his wife's bad behavior. It also showed that brains could sometimes overcome beauty and physical strength.

Below: Venus Receives Mars *by Italian painter Giovanni Battista Tiepolo (1696–1770). Venus and Mars were the Roman names for Aphrodite and Ares, whom Hephaestus punished for their affair.*

The Island of Lemnos

In Greek mythology, the Aegean island of Lemnos was associated with horrible smells. When the women of the island failed to honor Aphrodite, the love goddess cursed them with a foul bodily stench, which drove their husbands to seek alternative wives among the Thracians. The Lemnian women then murdered their husbands, and remained without men until the Argonauts stopped at the island. Either the Argonauts did not mind the women's smell, or, by the time they arrived, Aphrodite had shown forgiveness.

Another myth relates how a snake bit the archer Philoctetes, causing a wound that festered and began to smell badly. The odor, combined with Philoctetes' constant moaning, drove his comrades to maroon him on Lemnos, where he lived until he was rescued.

Hephaestus's smithy on Lemnos would have produced foul smells because of the chemicals used in metalworking. Today, doctors know that the toxicity of the materials used by blacksmiths (metalworkers) can cause a degenerative neurological disease that can lead to lameness. Hephaestus's physical condition may have reflected the fact that blacksmiths tended to become crippled after a number of years in their profession.

Above: The Temple of Hephaestus, Athens. The temple, which is older than the Parthenon (447–432 BCE), was dedicated to both Hephaestus and Athena as the patron and patroness of arts and crafts.

This was not the only occasion when Hephaestus was humiliated by the object of his desires. When Athena visited his smithy to ask for the god's assistance, Hephaestus chased after her. The virgin warrior goddess had no trouble fighting off the crippled blacksmith, but not before Hephaestus had ejaculated on her thigh. Athena wiped off the god's seed with a piece of wool and cast it on the earth, which was immediately impregnated, giving birth to the snake-footed Erichthonius. Two of Hephaestus's other children also inherited his lameness: the Argonaut Palaemonius and the club-wielding bandit Periphetes, whom the hero Theseus killed.

Cult of Hephaestus

It is likely that Hephaestus was originally a non-Greek deity. Herodotus named him as the father of a group of Phrygian gods called the Cabeiri, whose cult was practiced on the islands of the north Aegean. One reason that Lemnos became Hephaestus's main cult center could have been its once-active volcano—the island's inhabitants may have interpreted volcanic eruptions as the workings of Hephaestus in his smithy. Little is known about how

Hephaestus was worshiped. However, it is known that metalworking artisans observed the yearly festival of the Chalcheia, and every five years Athenians celebrated the Hephaestia in the god's honor, a festival that featured a torch race and rich sacrifices. The most complete and beautiful surviving temple in Athens belongs to Hephaestus. It stands on a hilltop overlooking the agora, or marketplace, which is fitting, for according to one account, Hephaestus taught humans his crafts and opened the way to commerce.

Hephaestus was not a favorite subject among artists. Besides vase paintings, the best known picture of him is by Dutch painter Maerten van Heemskerck (1498–1574), who in 1536 painted Aphrodite and Ares caught in the god's snare. In the picture, Hephaestus stands nearby holding a cane as the other Olympians look on.

KATHRYN CHEW

Bibliography

Graves, Robert. *The Greek Myths*. New York: Penguin USA, 1993.

Homer, and Robert Fagles, trans. *The Odyssey*. New York: Penguin USA, 1999.

SEE ALSO: Aphrodite; Ares; Athena; Cyclopes; Dionysus; Erichthonius; Graces, Helios; Hera; Heracles; Natural Forces; Pandora; Pelops; Philoctetes; Prometheus; Zeus.

HERA

Hera, the daughter of Cronus and Rhea, was queen of the Olympian gods. Her marriage to Zeus was troubled by his numerous infidelities, and many of the most celebrated Greek myths concern Hera's acts of vengeance against her husband, his mistresses, and their offspring.

Hera was queen of the Greek gods, and both sister and wife to Zeus. The goddess of women and marriage, she was one of the so-called 12 great Olympians; the others were Zeus, Aphrodite, Apollo, Ares, Artemis, Athena, Demeter, Dionysus, Hephaestus, Hermes, and Poseidon. The Romans later identified Hera with Juno.

As a mythical figure Hera is thought to have evolved from a prehistoric "great goddess" who was associated with the calendar year and with fertility. When the Pelasgians (early ancestors of the modern Greeks) first settled along the shores of the Mediterranean, their supreme male sky god, Zeus, merged forces with the local great goddess, who eventually became Hera.

Hera, the child of the Titans Cronus and Rhea, was born under a willow tree on the island of Samos. Cronus swallowed all his children at birth because he feared a prophecy that one of them would overthrow him. However, Rhea tricked him after the birth of their youngest child, Zeus, by replacing the baby with a wrapped stone and hiding him on the island of Crete. When Zeus grew to manhood he forced his father to disgorge the other children: Hestia, Hera, Demeter, Hades, and Poseidon. With their help, Zeus then defeated Cronus and became king of the gods.

Marriage

Zeus loved Hera and wanted to marry her, even though she was his sister. He courted her for a long time, but Hera showed little interest in him. Zeus then disguised himself as a bedraggled cuckoo on the summit of Mount Thornax. When Hera held the bird to her breast to warm it, Zeus resumed his real form and raped her. Because of this myth, the mountain was renamed Mount Kokkux, "Mount Cuckoo." Pregnant and ashamed, Hera agreed to marry Zeus. Their wedding took place on Crete. Annual celebrations were held at Hera's sanctuary in Argos to commemorate the event. The newlyweds spent a 300-year honeymoon on Samos. Hera

Left: This limestone head of Hera, dating from about 560 BCE, is now preserved in the Olympian Museum at Heraion, Greece.

never fully resigned herself to married life, however. To renew her virginity, she bathed yearly in the translucent, purifying waters of the Canathus Spring.

Described as "chief among the gods in beauty," "golden-shod," and "golden-throned," Hera was definitively regal. She was often depicted with a crown, a lotus-tipped scepter, and a pomegranate, which is a symbol of marriage. Her plant was the willow, and her sacred birds were the cuckoo, the hawk, the crow, and the peacock. Peacocks, symbols of pride, pulled her wagon. Hera's sacred animal was the cow; she was sometimes known as Bopis Hera ("cow-eyed Hera," later translated as "Hera with big eyes"). Hera's character represented womanhood in all its aspects. Temenus of Arcadia (a great-great grandson of Heracles) was said to have given Hera three names: Pais (girl or maiden); Teleia (grown-up or married); and Khera (widow).

Hera and Zeus had three children: Ares, Hebe, and Eileithyia. Ares, a terrifying, murderous god of war, was bloodstained, maniacal, and ever ready for battle. Hebe, the cupbearer of the gods, personified youth. She helped Hera to prepare her chariot, and washed Ares' wounds after he had been fighting. Eileithyia, the goddess of childbirth, was often identified with Fate and was sometimes said to be even older than her grandfather, Cronus.

When Zeus gave birth to the goddess Athena on his own, Hera was angry. She wanted to prove that she could do anything Zeus could do, so she alone produced Hephaestus and Typhon, although some sources claim Typhon was the son of Gaia. Hephaestus, a blacksmith who was the god of fire and the patron of craftsmen, was always represented as lame. There are two different accounts of his lameness. In one, Zeus quarreled with Hera and flung Hephaestus down from Olympus to the island of Lemnos for siding with her in the quarrel. In the other, Hephaestus

Hera's Battles with Other Gods

Hera quarreled with Poseidon over ownership of Argos, a city-state in the Peloponnese. The chief river, Inachus, declared that the land belonged to Hera, so Poseidon caused all rivers and springs to go dry. According to another version of the myth, the rivers chose Hera as their patron deity, so Poseidon made them disappear. These stories explained why the riverbeds in Argos remained dry except after rainfall.

In the Indian Wars of Dionysus, Hera sided against Artemis, so Artemis tried to shoot her. Hera wrapped herself in one of Zeus's clouds. Artemis shot arrow after arrow into the cloud until her quiver was empty, but caused Hera no injury. Hera then threw a frozen, jagged mass of hail, which broke Artemis's bow, defeating her.

Right: This Roman copy of an ancient Greek statue of Hera is displayed in the Pio-Clementine Museum in the Vatican City.

was born lame, and Hera, disgusted by his disability, flung him from Olympus. When Hephaestus became a man, he avenged himself on Hera by sending her a golden chair that trapped her when she sat in it. Hephaestus then refused to release her. According to some sources, Dionysus, the god of wine, got Hephaestus drunk to convince him to release Hera; other stories state that Hephaestus refused to set Hera free until she swore by the Styx River that she alone had created him.

Like Hephaestus, the monster Typhon had no father: Hera gave birth to him by invoking the powers of Heaven and Earth. Typhon's eyes dripped venom; his hundred horrible heads touched the stars, and red-hot lava poured from his gaping mouths. He tore up Mount Etna to throw it at the gods, but Zeus struck the mountain with a hundred thunderbolts and it fell back on to Typhon, trapping him inside. There he remained for eternity, belching fire, lava, and smoke—an explanation for the mountain's volcanic nature.

Love-hate relationship

Hera and Zeus had a stormy, complicated, and contradictory relationship. They did not trust each other. In one myth, Hera left Zeus after they argued. Zeus consulted Cithaeron, king of Plataea, who advised him to fake a new marriage: Zeus should dress a wooden female image and place it in a processional wagon. Zeus took his advice. In a rage, Hera approached the wagon, tore the dress from her rival, and found the image. Pleased at Zeus's effort to gain her attention, Hera was reconciled with him. The Daidala (meaning "wooden image") festival commemorated their reunion.

Zeus was jealous of Hera, too. When she complained that the centaur Ixion had tried to seduce her, he created a cloud in Hera's image and placed it on Ixion's bed. When Ixion raped the cloud, Zeus punished the centaur by tying him to a fiery, winged wheel to roll ceaselessly through the sky. On another occasion, Zeus made the giant Porphyrion fall in love with Hera, but as soon as Porphyrion approached her, Zeus struck him with a thunderbolt.

Contradictory behavior was a constant in the two Olympians' relationship. They argued about everything, including the question of whether men or women enjoyed sex more. Hera said that men did; Zeus maintained that it was women. Unable to agree, they consulted Tiresias, who had been a woman for seven years before being turned back into a man. He told them that women enjoyed sex nine times more than men. Hera was so annoyed by his

Above: The painting on this Greek ornamental jar (c. 580 BCE) shows Zeus and Hera on their way to be married.

answer that she struck Tiresias blind. Zeus then gave him the power of prophecy.

Despite their differences, Hera was proud of her relationship with Zeus. When Polytechnos, a Lydian carpenter, and Aedon, a daughter of Pandareus, boasted that their love for each other was greater than that between Hera and Zeus, Hera provoked them into a contest to see which of them could finish their work faster. The loser would give the winner a female slave. Aedon won because Hera had secretly helped her with her task. Polytechnos was infuriated. He raped Aedon's sister, Celidon, and then disguised her as the slave. The sisters discovered each other's identities, and in revenge they murdered Polytechnos's son, Itylus, and fed the boy to his father.

Zeus's love affairs

When Zeus had an affair with the gentle Leto, Hera relentlessly harassed the pregnant woman, partly because she knew that Leto would bear a son whom Zeus would love more than their own child, Ares. Leto gave birth to Artemis, who then delivered her own brother Apollo.

Io was another unfortunate mistress of Zeus. When Hera suspected their relationship, Zeus changed Io into a beautiful white heifer and denied the affair. Hera demanded the cow for herself as proof that he did not care for it. Zeus could not refuse, but later sent Hermes to steal the creature back. Meanwhile, however, Hera had set the hundred-eyed giant Argos to guard Io. Hermes killed Argos, but at that point Hera intervened: she placed Argos's eyes in the tail feathers of a peacock and sent a gadfly to pester Io for eternity. Io was finally able to resume her human shape in Egypt, where she gave birth to Epaphus. Hera tried to have the boy kidnapped, but Zeus saved him.

In another myth Zeus raped the nymph Callisto, a servant of the goddess Artemis, in whose honor she had promised to remain a virgin. According to one version of the story, Zeus changed Callisto into a bear to avoid detection by Hera. In another account, Hera changed Callisto into a bear in revenge. Hera then persuaded Artemis to shoot the pregnant Callisto. The arrow pierced Callisto's heart but Zeus managed to seize their baby, Arcas, from the dying body of his mistress. Zeus eventually installed both Callisto and Arcas in the heavens. Callisto

became the Great Bear constellation (Ursa Major or Big Dipper) and Arcas became the brilliant star Arcturus ("Bear guardian" or Little Dipper).

Hera's wrath could last for years. Zeus had an affair with Aegina, who then gave birth to a son, Aeacus. Hera waited until Aeacus was grown up before sending a serpent to poison the water of his native region. Many men died, drastically reducing the size of Aeacus's army. When Aeacus begged Zeus for help, he changed some nearby ants into men, thus foiling Hera's revenge.

Zeus's affair with Semele provoked a gruesome response from Hera. Zeus had sworn to give Semele anything she wanted, so Hera tricked Semele into asking Zeus to appear before her in his full glory. Zeus knew that no mortal could survive the experience, but he was unable to refuse her request. He appeared in his chariot, flashing lightning and thunder. Semele burst into flames. Zeus took their unborn child from her fire-scarred body and sewed it into his own thigh, from which he subsequently gave birth to Dionysus. Hermes took the boy to be raised by a mortal couple, Ino and Athamas. Determined to kill Dionysus, Hera drove the adoptive parents mad, causing them to kill their own children. Dionysus escaped only because Zeus changed him into a baby goat. Still Hera would not give up: she later drove Dionysus mad and forced him to wander Egypt and Syria.

Hera and Heracles

When Zeus fell for Alcmene, the beautiful wife of Amphitryon, the god disguised himself as her husband and ordered Helios to prolong the night to three times its usual length. During that night both Zeus and Amphitryon spent time with Alcmene, who became pregnant with twins. Zeus had foolishly boasted that the next child born in the line of Perseus would rule over Argos; Hera responded by making Eileithyia delay the birth of Heracles so that his cousin, Eurystheus, could be born first. Eurystheus duly became king of Mycenae.

However, Hera was still bent on revenge. When Heracles was eight months old she sent two huge serpents to kill him in his crib. The baby had superhuman strength, however, and squeezed them to death. When Heracles became an adult, Hera sent a fit of madness on him and he killed his wife and children. The Oracle at Delphi told Heracles that he could atone for his crime only by working for Eurystheus. The Mycenaean king ordered him to carry

Left: This painting by Italian artist Correggio (1494–1534) shows the seduction of Io by Zeus.

Familial Battlefield

According to Homer in Book Five of his epic poem the *Iliad*, written around the eighth century BCE, Hera and Athena joined forces against Ares because he had promised them that he would fight for the Greeks, but instead sided with their enemies the Trojans. Hera and Athena rode in Hera's chariot to Mount Olympus, where they asked Zeus for permission to rid the battlefield of Ares.

Zeus agreed to their request, and the two goddesses rode back down to the battlefield. There Athena assured the great Greek warrior Diomedes that he could strike Ares without fear, because she would be by his side. Diomedes wounded Ares as the invisible Athena guided his spear, and Ares retreated to Olympus. Ares complained to Zeus, but he received short shrift from his father, who called him "the most hateful to me of all Olympians," and blamed his fractious nature on his heredity:

"This beastly, incorrigible truculence of yours," Zeus told Ares, "comes from your mother, Hera, whom I keep but barely in my power, no matter what I say to her."

Right: This Roman statue depicts the infant Heracles preparing to deal with one of the snakes sent by Hera to kill him.

out 12 great labors. Even while Heracles was trying to perform these tasks, Hera continued to oppose him. One of the labors involved fetching the belt of Hippolyte, the Amazon queen. Hippolyte volunteered to give her belt to Heracles, but Hera, disguised as a woman in the crowd, shouted that Heracles intended to kidnap the monarch, so the Amazons armed themselves. Seeing that, Heracles jumped to the conclusion that Hippolyte had tricked him, so he killed her. Another labor required Heracles to round up the cattle of Geryon. Again Hera interfered, sending a gadfly to disperse the beasts into the mountains. Heracles caught some of them and brought them back to Eurystheus as a sacrifice intended to appease Hera.

Hera was not placated, however. As Heracles returned to Greece from Troy, Hera sent storms that forced his ship aground on the island of Kos, where he was almost killed. Later Heracles restored Tyndareos as king of Sparta by battling Hippocoon the Usurper and his 13 sons. During this adventure, the hero found that, for almost the first time in his life, Hera had not opposed him. In gratitude, he founded a sanctuary in Sparta for her and sacrificed goats in

her honor. When Zeus made Heracles immortal, Hera relented and allowed Heracles to marry her daughter Hebe.

Most of the myths about Zeus and Hera have the same basic plot: he pursues a mortal female, mates with her, and then attempts to hide the relationship from his wife. A child is born, and Hera causes grief to mother and baby. There are two exceptions to this rule. Zeus's affair with Aphrodite was unique because she was the only other Olympian with whom he ever consorted. In his encounter with the witch Iynx, Zeus was the quarry not the hunter: he was seduced while under her spell. True to form, Hera responded violently to both infidelities. She tried to disfigure Priapus, Zeus's son by Aphrodite, while he was still in his mother's womb, and she turned Iynx to stone.

Injured pride

Many myths show that Hera's pride was easily wounded, and she punished women who believed that their beauty rivaled hers. She caused the three daughters of the giant Proitos to roam throughout Argos because they had not worshiped her image in the required manner. She threw Orion's first

wife, Side, into Hades because she claimed to be as beautiful as the goddess herself. When a flawlessly beautiful Pygmaioi girl named Oinoe showed no reverence for Hera, the goddess turned her into a crane. After the transformation, Oinoe still yearned to see her child Mopsos, so she kept flying over the Pygmaioi with her long neck outstretched. The Pygmaioi tried to chase away the irritating crane, a response that led to a perpetual state of war between the Pygmaioi and the birds.

Hera and Jason

When Pelias, king of Iolcus in Thessaly, murdered his stepmother in Hera's shrine, the goddess was offended and determined to destroy him. Pelias was a usurper. As the rightful heir, his nephew Jason, was on his way to claim the throne, Hera, disguised as an old woman, asked him to carry her over the Anaurus River. During the crossing Jason lost a sandal. When he reached Iolcus, Pelias, who had never previously met the boy, knew who he was because an oracle had told him that he would be dethroned by a "one-sandaled man." In an attempt to avert his fate, and inspired by Hera, who put the idea into his head, Pelias told Jason that he would willingly surrender the kingdom if Jason

Below: German artist Franz von Stuck (1863–1928) created this painting, The Three Goddesses: Athena, Hera, and Aphrodite *(1922).*

Above: Worship of Hera was not confined to Greece. This temple to the goddess is at Paestum, near Naples, Italy.

would steal the Golden Fleece from Colchis, a land on the east coast of the Black Sea (part of modern Georgia). That was generally acknowledged to be an impossible task, but Hera helped Jason and his 50 companions throughout their adventure, at one point guiding their ship, *Argo,* through the impassable Clashing Rocks, huge cliffs that constantly crashed together. When Jason returned to Iolcus in triumph with the Fleece, he was accompanied by the witch Medea, who—as Hera knew—was fated to destroy Pelias.

Hera and the Judgment of Paris

When Peleus, king of Phthia married the sea goddess Thetis, all the Olympian deities were invited to the wedding except Eris, the goddess of discord. In revenge, she appeared for an instant and threw down among the guests a golden apple, on which was inscribed "To the Fairest." Hera, Athena, and Aphrodite all vied for the fruit. When there was no outright winner, they appealed to Zeus, but he did not want to choose between them himself, so he sent them to Paris, the son of King Priam of Troy, who at the time was living as a shepherd, unaware of his royal birth. Each of the goddesses tried to bribe him: Athena promised him victory in war, Hera promised to make him king of all men, and Aphrodite promised him the most beautiful woman in the world. Paris chose Aphrodite, only to find that his prize, Helen, was already married to Menelaus, king of Sparta. Paris then abducted Helen and took her back with him to Troy. Menelaus assembled a

great army to retrieve his wife, and the Trojan War began. Hera aligned herself against Paris and the Trojans. She schemed and battled throughout the war on behalf of the Greeks, and even tricked Aphrodite into seducing Zeus in order to distract him from supporting the Trojans.

Popular goddess

Revered in every home, Hera was immensely popular in ancient Greece. Her temples, known as Heraion, were built throughout the country; the most important were at Argos, Samos, and Olympia. Her games at Olympia, called the Heraia, were foot races for unmarried women, staggered according to age groups, with the youngest setting off first. In many ways the Heraia were similar to the Olympic Games: every event-winner received a crown of olive branches and a portion of a sacrificed cow. Women ran with their hair down, their right shoulders bare, and wearing short tunics cut above their knees.

ALYS CAVINESS

Bibliography

Bulfinch, Thomas. *Bulfinch's Mythology.* New York: Modern Library, 1998.

Hesiod, and M. L. West, trans. *Theogony; and Works and Days.* New York: Oxford University Press, 1999.

Homer, and Robert Fagles, trans. *The Iliad.* New York: Penguin USA, 2003.

Howatson, M. C., and Ian Chilvers. *Concise Oxford Companion to Classical Literature.* New York: Oxford University Press, 1993.

SEE ALSO: Aphrodite; Ares; Athena; Callisto; Cronus; Dionysus; Greece; Hebe; Helen; Hephaestus; Heracles; Jason; Juno; Paris; Tiresias; Typhon; Zeus.

HERACLES

A national hero of ancient Greece, Heracles performed a series of arduous labors, and his name became a byword for physical strength and bravery. He was worshiped as a god in Greece from at least the sixth century BCE, and his cult was probably the earliest nonindigenous form of worship accepted in Rome.

Heracles was one of the greatest of all ancient mythological heroes. His amazing exploits and accomplishments took place over an enormous geographical area that stretched beyond his native land into the farthest corners of the known world. Unlike the deeds of lesser figures, his actions benefited all of Greece rather than just one particular region or city, and Heracles is therefore sometimes described as "panhellenic." He destroyed or subdued a host of monsters. Even the gods marveled at his enormous strength. Numerous kings, emperors, and generals appropriated Heracles' two most distinctive symbols—the lion skin and the club—in order to associate themselves with the hero in the hope that they might bask in some of his reflected glory.

The main source for the story of the labors of Heracles is the second-century BCE mythographer Apollodorus, but he is also mentioned by much earlier authors, including Homer (c. eighth–ninth century BCE). In the *Odyssey*, Homer describes how Odysseus meets Heracles' spirit in the underworld. For the Greeks he personified superhuman courage and strength. His life was one of toil and hardship on behalf of humankind; his reward was to become immortal after his death.

Heracles became the object of cult worship in Greece, where his rituals involved feasting and sacrifice. Animals

Right: This sculpture of Heracles is an ancient Roman copy of a Greek original dating from the fourth century BCE.

were lifted onto the sacrificial altar in an echo of Heracles' great feats of strength. At Thebes in Boeotia the temple of Heracles was attached to a gymnasium, in commemoration of the hero's athletic prowess.

Circumstances of his birth

Heracles was the son of Zeus and Alcmene, a descendant of Perseus and the wife of Amphitryon. While Amphitryon was away at war, Zeus came to Alcmene disguised as her husband. To satisfy his lust, the god caused the night to stretch out to three times its normal length. On the same night, however, Alcmene's husband returned and also had intercourse with her. As a result she became pregnant with two male children, one the semidivine Heracles, the other the mortal Iphicles. Most ancient writers say that Heracles was born at Thebes, because that is where Amphitryon lived, but in some accounts he is linked with Argos, which was Alcmene's family's home. Some mythographers suggest that Heracles—"glory of Hera"—was so named to appease the wrath of Zeus's wife, who was jealous of the children that Zeus had through other females.

It was Hera who caused most of Heracles' subsequent troubles. Zeus had foolishly boasted that the next child born in the line of Perseus would rule over Argos; Hera responded by making her daughter, Eileithyia, goddess of childbirth, delay the birth of Heracles so that his cousin, Eurystheus, could be born first (and prematurely). Alcmene eventually carried her twins for a painful 10 months. Even so, after Heracles was born some of the other goddesses tricked Hera into briefly suckling the baby with her own milk in order to ensure his immortality. When he clamped down too hard on her nipple, however, Hera yanked him away, and the spurting milk formed the Milky Way.

After the baby was returned to his mother, Hera sent serpents into his nursery to try to kill him. Since she was unsure which of the two newborn children belonged to Zeus, she sent two snakes to kill both twins. The mortal baby began to cry when he saw the danger, but Heracles grabbed both snakes and strangled them. The parents were shocked when they rushed into the room. They knew then that they had a supernatural child who possessed fantastic strength, and they decided that he deserved a special education. The best teachers were appointed, one of whom was Linus. While Heracles excelled in the more physically demanding arts, such as archery and wrestling, he failed miserably at music, Linus's specialty. One day, when Linus was ridiculing Heracles for being clumsy and incompetent, the boy picked up the instrument that he was playing and struck Linus over the head with it, killing him.

The 12 Labors of Heracles

1. Skinning the Nemean Lion.
2. Killing the Hydra of Lerna.
3. Capturing the Arcadian stag.
4. Capturing the Erymanthion boar.
5. Cleaning the Augean stables.
6. Shooting the birds of the Stymphalian marshes.
7. Capturing the Cretan bull.
8. Capturing the human-eating horses of Diomedes.
9. Obtaining the belt of the Amazon queen Hippolyte.
10. Driving the cattle of Geryon from the far west to Greece.
11. Fetching the golden apples of the Hesperides.
12. Capturing Cerberus, the three-headed watchdog of the underworld.

Right:
This Greek vase from the eighth century BCE depicts Heracles wrestling with the Nemean lion.

Early feats

Heracles' parents feared his temper and his strength, so they sent him off into the country to tend the flocks on Mount Cithaeron, between Thebes and Thespiae (ruled by Thespius). The boy grew tall and continued to show signs of exceptional athleticism. He killed a ferocious lion with his bare hands. This so impressed King Thespius that he invited Heracles to stay in his palace and dine with him. Thespius and the Thespians, meanwhile, were suffering at the hands of Erginus, king of nearby Orchomenus, who was demanding from them a heavy tribute. Thespius was secretly hoping to strengthen his kingdom by having the powerful Heracles produce children with his daughters. At the dinner party, Thespius got Heracles drunk on wine, then sent him in to his daughters—all 50 of them. Heracles had intercourse with every one, producing a child through each union. Soon afterward, when envoys from King Erginus came to Thespiae to exact the tribute, Heracles cut off their ears and noses, hung them around their necks, and sent the envoys packing back to Orchomenus. This sparked the outbreak of a war between the two states, but with Heracles fighting on the side of the Thespians and rearming them with weapons stored in a temple, the Thespians prevailed and began to exact their own tribute from the Minyans of Orchomenus.

Soon Heracles married Megara of Thebes, and they had several children together, all of whom he loved very much. Hera, however, was not content to let the hero lead a happy life. She sent a fit of madness on him, and he began to slay everyone in his family, either by throwing them into a fire or by shooting them with arrows. The only way that Heracles could atone for these murders was by submitting to his cousin Eurystheus, who set him 10 tasks. Because Heracles cheated on two of the original tasks, the number was later increased to 12.

The first 10 labors of Heracles

The first labor Eurystheus ordered Heracles to perform was to kill the Nemean lion, which was not a normal lion but a creature born from monstrous parents and brother to the famous Sphinx of Thebes. For years it had ravaged the land around Nemea in the Peloponnese, where it lived in a cave with two exits. Because its hide was invulnerable, Heracles could not harm it with his arrows. So he fashioned a club for himself, and used it to drive the lion into its cave, where he had blocked up one of the exits. He then strangled the beast with his bare hands. He used the dead lion's own claws to flay its skin, which from then on he wore as a distinctive coat and helmet.

Eurystheus never liked Heracles, and the hero's slaying of the Nemean lion only made him fear and loathe him more. The second labor that he imposed on Heracles was to kill the Hydra, a giant, multiheaded, snakelike creature that spewed venom from its mouth. Even the breath that

Below: This statue by French sculptor François-Joseph Bosio (1768–1845) depicts Heracles slaying the monstrous Hydra, the second of his 12 labors.

Heracles and Antaeus

Heracles encountered Antaeus on the way back to Greece from his 11th labor in the garden of the Hesperides, which was situated in the far west of the known world. Antaeus, a son of the earth goddess Gaia, was a giant who challenged every traveler he met to a wrestling contest. He had never lost a fight, and he had killed all his previous adversaries.

When Heracles and Antaeus came to grips, the hero soon discovered that, no matter how many times he threw Antaeus off and tossed him to the ground, he derived no advantage from his opponent's falls. On the contrary, the giant appeared to draw even greater strength from every throw. Heracles eventually deduced that the giant derived his power from contact with the earth, which was his mother, so he held Antaeus aloft until all his power had drained away, and then strangled him.

After Heracles had disposed of Antaeus, he proceeded safely back to his taskmaster and cousin, King Eurystheus of Argos, to receive instructions for his final labor.

Right: This painting by Antonio Pollaiuolo (c.1431–1498) depicts Heracles grappling with the giant Antaeus. Heracles defeated his opponent by lifting him from the ground and strangling him.

issued from it while it slept was poisonous enough to kill anyone nearby. The Hydra lived in Lerna, a swampy area of the Peloponnese. When he confronted the monster, Heracles discovered that every time he cut off one of the Hydra's heads, two would grow back in its place. He ordered his nephew, Iolaus, to sear the neck-stumps whenever he cut off a head, so that new ones would not be able to grow back. After successfully beheading the monster of its many heads, Heracles discovered that the middle head was immortal. He took a huge rock and buried the head beneath it, after which he dipped his arrows into the Hydra's venomous blood. Because Heracles used the services of his nephew Iolaus, this labor did not count toward the 10 that he needed to complete.

Heracles' third labor involved capturing the golden-horned stag of Ceryneia. This creature was extremely swift, though it was larger than a bull. The collar that it wore around its neck bore a legend saying that it was dedicated to Artemis, meaning that it would be an act of great impiety to hunt it. As in the case of the boar, deer often symbolize the rite of passage from childhood to adulthood. Heracles chased the stag for a full year until finally he was able to get close enough to wound it, then catch it. As Heracles returned to Argos, Artemis and her brother Apollo stopped him and tried to wrestle the animal away from

him. They relented only after Heracles explained to them that he was merely following the orders of Eurystheus and that he would not harm the deer.

Next, as a fourth labor, Eurystheus ordered Heracles to bring back alive the monstrous Erymanthion boar. The creature haunted the slopes of Mount Erymanthus and was causing considerable havoc in the countryside. (Boars in myth often symbolize the passage of young boys into manhood.) Heracles managed to drive the Erymanthian boar into deep snow, throw a net over it, and carry it back to Eurystheus. The king, terrified by the sight of the boar, hid in a huge pot in the ground.

As a fifth labor, Eurystheus ordered Heracles to clean the stables of Augeas, the king of Elis in the western Peloponnese. Augeas's father had given him great herds of cattle, but Augeas had failed to clean up their dung. As a result, the countryside was being deprived of fertilizer and therefore becoming infertile. Heracles went to Augeas and arranged a deal by which he would be paid for cleaning out all the dung. He then diverted a nearby river to run through the stable and thereby cleaned it thoroughly. When Heracles went back to Augeas for his money, Augeas refused to pay him on the grounds that the river had done the work, not Heracles. Eurystheus was unwilling to count this as one of the original 10 labors, since Heracles had asked for money. Later, Heracles returned to punish Augeas, whom he eventually killed. During that adventure, near Elis at Olympia, Heracles founded the Olympian Games.

The sixth labor that Eurystheus imposed on Heracles was to rid Lake Stymphalus of a huge flock of birds that were devouring everything in sight and making excessive noise. Some ancient authors say that their droppings were acidic and that they would shoot their metal-tipped feathers at passersby. Heracles used castanets to drive the birds from hiding and then downed them with his arrows, the tips of which were steeped in Hydra venom.

For his seventh labor, Heracles was ordered to bring back alive the bull of Crete. This was the white bull that Poseidon had sent to King Minos but which Minos had failed to sacrifice to him in return. Heracles captured the bull and swam with it from Crete to mainland Greece. After showing it to Eurystheus, he tried to dedicate it to Hera, but the goddess, still angry, refused the gift.

Eurystheus then told Heracles that, for his eighth labor, he must capture the mares of Diomedes, king of the savage Thracians, and bring them back alive to him. The four horses were unique in that they lived on human flesh. Heracles was able to tame the animals by feeding Diomedes himself to them. After they had eaten their fill, it was no problem to lead them back to Argos. By overcoming Minos and Diomedes, Heracles had subdued the closest and most fearsome leaders of the Greeks' rivals.

It was during the eighth labor that Heracles visited the town of Pherae in Thessaly. There he met Admetus on the very day that his wife, Alcestis, had died. When Heracles discovered that the couple had entered a compact by which the wife would die in her husband's place, the hero wrestled Thanatos (Death) and stole Alcestis back, returning her to the selfish and now embarrassed Admetus.

The ninth labor of Heracles involved stealing the girdle or belt of Hippolyte, the queen of the Amazons. The Amazons were a tribe of women warriors who lived on the southern shore of the Black Sea. Although Hippolyte willingly agreed to give Heracles the girdle, the vengeful Hera caused a misunderstanding between them, and Heracles slew Hippolyte. The Amazons attacked, but during the battle, Heracles took so many hostages that the Amazons were forced to trade the belt for them.

For his 10th labor, Heracles was sent to retrieve the cattle of Geryon, a three-bodied giant, from a distant island either in the far reaches of the Mediterranean Sea or in the Atlantic Ocean. In order to traverse the vast ocean, Heracles borrowed from Helios, the

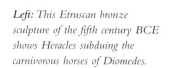

Left: This Etruscan bronze sculpture of the fifth century BCE shows Heracles subduing the carnivorous horses of Diomedes.

sun god, the cup in which he returned to the east after sunset every evening. When Heracles reached the island, he struck down Orthus, Geryon's two-headed guard dog, with a single blow of his club, then slew the giant with his arrows. After returning to Europe in Helios's cup, Heracles then drove the cattle all the way through Spain, Gaul (modern France), Italy, and on to Greece.

The final two labors

Heracles then went back to Argos to receive instructions from Eurystheus about his two additional tasks. For his 11th labor he had to travel to the western extremity of the world and bring back some golden apples. The tree on which they grew was tended by the Hesperides, daughters of Atlas. They had been set to look after the tree by Hera, who had been given it by Gaia as a wedding present. The golden apples of the Hesperides were guarded by Ladon, an immortal dragon with a hundred heads. Heracles traveled across northern Africa on his way to Mount Atlas. At some point during this journey, he met up with Prometheus and freed him from his captivity, during which he had been constantly gnawed by Zeus's eagle. In Libya Heracles encountered the giant Antaeus (see box, page 661), who wrestled and killed everyone he met. Antaeus was invincible so long as he was attached to the earth. Heracles lifted him on his shoulders and choked him to death.

Some ancient writers recount that on his way to the garden Heracles visited Atlas and agreed to hold up the sky while the Titan went to retrieve the apples. When Atlas

Heracles in Art

The oldest surviving artistic depictions of Heracles date from the ninth century BCE. Hundreds of vases and bowls of the period depict the hero's everyday life as well as his 12 labors.

In many of the scenes showing Heracles fighting the Nemean lion, Athena is in the background to reassure the viewer of the hero's ultimate victory. Although the beast was supposedly invulnerable to weapons, Heracles is often shown attacking it with a club.

Another commonly depicted labor is the theft of the girdle of Hippolyte. There are nearly 400 examples, in some of which Heracles is killing the Amazon queen. The 11th labor is usually represented, not by the theft of the golden apples, but by Heracles seated before Atlas asking for his help.

Most of the images relating to the fourth labor show Heracles presenting the Erymanthion boar to Eurystheus, who is hiding in a vase.

Right: This sculpture of Heracles with the Erymanthion boar is by the Flemish-Italian artist Giovanni Bologna (1529–1608), commonly known as Giambologna. The 12 labors of Heracles have been a popular subject for artists for many centuries.

Above: Heracles on the Pyre *is one of a series of paintings depicting the deeds of Heracles by Italian artist Guido Reni (1575–1642).*

returned, he decided that he wanted to take the apples to Eurystheus himself, and so refused to take the sky back on his shoulders. Heracles pretended to agree to this plan, and asked only that Atlas hold up the sky while he shifted his shoulders into a more comfortable position. When Atlas held the sky once more, Heracles grabbed the apples and promptly departed. Other accounts say that Heracles found the garden, slew the dragon, and retrieved the apples by himself. After Heracles showed the apples to Eurystheus, Athena returned them to the garden of Hera.

For the 12th labor Heracles had to descend into the underworld and bring out Cerberus, the three-headed guard dog of the underworld. In the underworld Heracles came across the imprisoned Theseus and Peirithous, two heroes who had tried to kidnap Persephone, the queen of the underworld. The goddess permitted Heracles to free Theseus, who was stuck in the chair of forgetfulness, but not Peirithous. Then Heracles grabbed Cerberus and dragged him up to Eurystheus. When Eurystheus saw the dog, he again took fright and jumped into his clay pot for safety. The dog was then returned to its master, Hades.

Life after labors

After the last of his labors, Heracles had finally atoned for the murder of his family. It was by no means the end of his adventures, however. He mounted many expeditions against various enemies, including the Trojans (Heracles lived one generation before the Trojan War), Augeas, and the people of Pylos (in the Peloponnese) and Sparta. He came into contact with Priam and Nestor, who were in the twilight of their lives when the Trojan War began.

While in the underworld, Heracles had promised the Greek prince Meleager that, when he went back to the world above, Heracles would marry his sister, Deianeira of Calydon. When Heracles returned, he headed for Calydon, where he found Deianeira being wooed by the river god Achelous, who was able to turn himself into any creature. When Deianeira expressed the desire to marry Heracles instead of Achelous, the two suitors became locked in mortal combat. In the end Heracles defeated Achelous while the latter was in the form of a bull. Heracles ripped off one of his horns, at which point Achelous admitted defeat and conceded the hand of Deianeira to Heracles.

Later, Heracles won a girl named Iole in an archery contest. Because her father refused to hand her over to Heracles, the hero had to take her by force. According to some versions, he killed her father. Most versions agree that in a fit of madness he killed her brother, who may have been one of his supporters, and so had to pay for his sins

again. The oracle at Delphi was so appalled by his repeated crime that she refused to tell him what to do. Heracles became enraged, took the tripod of the Pythian priestess, and threatened to set up his own oracle. Apollo arrived, and he and Heracles came to blows until Zeus unleashed a thunderbolt to separate them. The oracle then told Heracles that to purify himself he must become a slave of Omphale, queen of Lydia, for three years. This was a humiliation for Heracles, because Omphale dressed him in women's clothes and took his lion skin and club for herself. Heracles even learned weaving from the queen.

Deianeira, meanwhile, had become jealous that Heracles might love Iole more than her. One day, while Heracles and his wife were crossing a dangerous river, a centaur named Nessus appeared and offered Deianeira a lift on his back to the further bank. Once on land, Nessus assaulted Deianeira. Heracles, on seeing what was happening, shot one of his poisonous arrows into Nessus. Before Nessus died he told Deianeira to take some of his blood because it had special qualities: "If ever Heracles begins to lose affection for you," he told her, "this blood can be used to restore his love." It was a trick, since the blood had been tainted by the venomous arrows. When Deianeira finally decided to act, she rubbed some of the supposed love-potion on a shirt and sent it to Heracles to wear. When he put it on, the fiery acid burned his skin. When he could bear the agony no longer, Heracles built a funeral pyre for himself and climbed on top. He begged servants and passersby to set fire to the wood, but no one would until a certain Philoctetes wandered by and lit it. As a reward, Heracles gave him his unerring bow and arrows. In some mysterious way, the fire only purged Heracles of his mortal parts, so that with a clap of thunder and the descent of a cloud, Heracles was lifted up to heaven to live with the gods there. In some versions of the myth, the mortal side of Heracles dwelled with the other shades in the underworld. The now divine Heracles was reconciled once and for all with Hera, and married Hebe, the goddess of youthfulness.

KIRK SUMMERS

Bibliography

Apollodorus, and Robin Hard, trans. *The Library of Greek Mythology.* New York: Oxford University Press, 1999.

Bulfinch, Thomas. *Bulfinch's Mythology.* New York: Modern Library, 1998.

Graves, Robert. *The Greek Myths.* New York: Penguin USA, 1993.

SEE ALSO: Amazons; Atlas; Crete; Hades; Hera; Hesperides; Hippolyte; Zeus.

HERMAPHRODITUS

In Greek myth, Hermaphroditus was the child of Hermes, the messenger of the gods, and the love goddess Aphrodite. His story—which reflects Greek ideas about gender and marriage—relates how he took on both male and female sexual characteristics.

Hermaphroditus was the only child of Hermes and Aphrodite, born after Zeus took pity on the messenger of the gods' unrequited love for the goddess. Zeus sent an eagle to steal one of Aphrodite's sandals and give it to Hermes. When Aphrodite came to recover it, he won her love and she bore him a beautiful son, whose name combined both of theirs.

The first full account of Hermaphroditus's story occurs in the epic poem *Metamorphoses* by Roman poet Ovid (43 BCE–c. 17 CE). Ovid relates that Hermaphroditus grew up in the caves of Mount Ida, southeast of Troy, in the care of nymphs. When he was 15 years old he set out to travel the world. On his journey he came to a pool where he met another nymph, Salmacis. She instantly fell in love with Hermaphroditus, but he rejected her. Then, as he began to swim in the pool, Salmacis threw herself upon him and embraced him so forcefully that boy and nymph melted together into one body, which was therefore androgynous—both male and female. After the change, Hermaphroditus prayed to his parents that the pool—located near Halicarnassus, one of the ancient cities where Hermes and Aphrodite were both worshiped together—should cause any other man who swam in it to become similarly androgynous.

Worship of Hermaphroditus

Evidence that people worshiped Hermaphroditus as a god comes from a fourth-century-BCE inscription, which records a woman named Phano making a dedication to him "in prayer." A later source refers to a sanctuary of Hermaphroditus in the countryside near Athens: it mentions that a woman brought to it an offering of woven flowers. From the third century BCE onward, figurines of Hermaphroditus were fairly numerous in the Greek world. They were installed as decorations in gymnasia, baths, and theaters, and were also placed in graves and left in sanctuaries as dedications.

Right: This second-century-BCE statue depicts Hermaphroditus sleeping. The mattress and pillow were added in the 17th century.

The earliest written reference to Hermaphroditus occurs in Greek philosopher Theophrastus's (c. 372–c. 287 BCE) *Characters*, in which he portrays various types of eccentric people. According to Theophrastus, on the fourth day of the month, the "superstitious man crowns the hermaphroditus" in his house. It is possible that the use of the word *hermaphroditus* refers to a sculpture of Aphrodite in the form of a herm, a square pillar with a deity's head at the top. However, scholars believe that Theophrastus was referring to the mythical character, who was invoked in a sacred ritual.

Hermaphroditus and marriage

Theophrastus's account also suggests a link between Hermaphroditus and the institution of marriage. The reference to the "fourth day of the month" is telling: this was the luckiest day to hold a wedding. Hermaphroditus's association with marriage seems to have been that, by embodying both masculine and feminine qualities, he or she symbolized the coming together of men and women in sacred union. Various marriage rituals involving switching genders emphasized this fusion of the sexes. On the island of Kos, for instance, the bridegroom wore women's clothes, while in Sparta it was the brides who dressed like men. In Argos the marriage ritual was even more pronounced— brides wore false beards. The thinking behind these customs appears to have been that the bride and groom could switch roles since, in the union of their marriage, one became indistinguishable from the other.

Another factor linking Hermaphroditus to weddings was his or her parents' role in protecting and blessing brides. Hermes and Aphrodite were worshiped together in a number of Greek sanctuaries, and they were sometimes represented as a pair, most notably in the early fifth-century-BCE terra-cotta statuettes from the sanctuary of Persephone in Epizephyrian Locri in southern Italy. These statuettes were almost certainly dedicated by women on the occasion of their marriage, in the expectation of the deities' joint blessing. Aphrodite's importance to brides stemmed from her role as the deity of love and mature sexuality, and as the patroness of the mutual attraction of marriage partners. In Greek weddings a woman known as the *nympheutria* impersonated Aphrodite during the ceremony, accompanying the bride and helping her to assume her new sexual role and social position. Roman weddings followed a similar custom, with the part of the Roman love goddess, Venus, played by a woman called a *pronuba*.

Hermes was significant for brides for quite different reasons. Besides his role as the messenger of the gods, he was the deity of boundary crossings and rituals that marked the transfer from one condition to another, particularly at funerals and weddings. The Greeks believed that Hermes

patronized the social aspect of marriage, symbolized by the transfer of the bride from her father's house to her husband's. In classical depictions of wedding scenes, Hermes is portrayed leading the wedding procession.

Greek views about gender

The myth of Hermaphroditus touches on the sexual differences between men and women—a notion that, for the Greeks, was both highly important and ambiguous. Early Greek sources suggest a fundamental distinction between the genders. In *Theogony*, for example, the eighth-century BCE-Greek poet Hesiod's account of the origins of the gods, the first union was between the male Uranus (sky) and the female Gaia (earth). Writings produced by followers of the Orphic mystery religion, based on the teaching and songs of the Greek hero Orpheus, similarly describe a union between a male and female deity at the creation of the world. According to an Orphic account by the fifth-century-BCE Greek writer Pherecydes of Syros, the world began with the marriage of Zas, the high god and maker of order, to Chthonie, the goddess of earth. As a wedding gift, Zas gave Chthonie a robe on which was embroidered the entire universe.

For the Greeks, gender differences prefigured social differences. People believed that men reached their perfect condition as philosopher-king while women achieved this state through marriage. Furthermore, men were in charge of government while women asserted their powers in the home and through the performance of certain rituals. Any variance from these rules—for instance, a cowardly man or a woman in authority—challenged the social and cosmic order. A creature belonging to both sexes was, therefore, profoundly threatening to this way of thinking. Yet one aspect of the Hermaphroditus myth directly reflected real life—the birth of dimorphic children, with male and female sexual characteristics. Today, dimorphic humans, plants, and animals are called hermaphrodites for the Greek myth. Roman sources report that, during the third, second, and first centuries BCE, there were large numbers of such births. People perceived dimorphic children to be dangerous monsters and evil omens.

Androgyny in Greek society

To say that the Greeks were afraid of anyone who merged the characteristics of male and female does not explain why people worshiped Hermaphroditus and represented him or her in their works of art. One reason for honoring Hermaphroditus was that he or she represented in extreme form what people could aspire to only moderately. In other words, the fusing together of Hermaphroditus and Salmacis dramatically symbolized the act of sexual union. The extreme aspect of Hermaphroditus also suggests why people worshiped him or her alongside Pan, the god of the wild countryside, and the river god Achelous—fertile, erratic, and sometimes dangerous figures that evoked the powers of nature. Similarly, in classical art, Hermaphroditus is depicted in the company of the wild, part-human, part-animal satyrs and fauns.

Another explanation for Hermaphroditus's popularity was the role androgyny played in Greek society. Besides wedding ceremonies, a number of other rituals involved people of one sex taking on the dress and behavior of

Left: Salmacis and Hermaphroditus *(c. 1581), by Flemish artist Bartholomeus Spranger (1546–1611), depicts the nymph spying on the bathing god.*

Above: This first-century-CE wall painting from the Roman city of Pompeii depicts the notoriously lustful Pan fleeing from the beckoning Hermaphrodite.

members of the opposite sex. In the Athenian ritual honoring the voyage of Theseus and his companions to Crete, where the hero slew the Minotaur, young men acted the parts of girls who had accompanied Theseus. At Argos, during the annual festival called the Hybristika, the "festival of outrage," all the participants dressed as the other sex. The events in both Athens and Argos were ceremonies of disorder—similar to carnivals such as Mardi Gras and to Halloween—where order was broken only to be strengthened by its restoration. Transvestism (dressing and acting like the opposite sex) was also frequent in rituals celebrating Dionysus, the god of wine, intoxication, and the theater. Athens held several dramatic festivals each year in which an image of the god had the seat of honor among the audience. Generally women were not permitted to take part in Greek drama, so in performances during these festivals all the women's parts were played by men.

Androgyny also appears in an acceptable light in a variety of Greek myths. For example, the heroes Achilles and Heracles both spent time in women's clothing— Achilles in the female quarters of the palace of Lycomedes, king of Scyros; Heracles in the company of Queen Omphale of Lydia. The myth of Tiresias, the seer from Thebes, relates how he became a woman after hitting two snakes. Seven years later he struck the same snakes again and returned to being a man. He thus had an understanding of the inner thoughts of both men and women. This led Zeus and Hera to consult him in an argument over which gender gained the most pleasure from sex. Caenis was a beautiful woman who was raped by the sea-god Poseidon. He then granted her wish that she might never be raped again by turning her into a man. After this transformation Caenis took the name Caeneus.

JAMES M. REDFIELD

Bibliography

Hesiod, and M. L. West, trans. *Theogony; and Works and Days*. New York: Oxford University Press, 1999.

Ovid, and A. D. Melville, trans. *Metamorphoses*. New York: Oxford University Press, 1998.

SEE ALSO: Achilles; Aphrodite; Crete; Dionysus; Festivals; Heracles; Hermes; Nymphs; Orpheus; Theseus; Tiresias.

HERMES

Hermes was the messenger of the Greek gods, and he was often sent on errands by his father, Zeus. At times he was mischievous and thieved, but he was also a divine guide who led other gods and mortals from harm to safety. One of his most important roles was as god of boundaries. A herm, named for Hermes, was a stone square pillar the Greeks would erect to mark the boundary between properties. Hermes was known as Mercury by the Romans.

Above: This Roman sculpture of Hermes, whom the Romans called Mercury, was made in the second century BCE and is a copy of a fifth-century-BCE Greek original. It depicts Hermes with a beard, but most later depictions have him without one and appearing younger than he does here.

Although Hermes is described in many myths as having been one of the youngest of the gods, historically he was not a latecomer to the Greek pantheon. His name appears in early inscriptions from the time of the Mycenaean Greeks, who first inhabited mainland Greece around 1500–1100 BCE. Specifically, Hermes is listed on tablets in Linear B, the ancient Mycenaean writing system, as one of the gods to whom tribute was owed.

Despite being one of the youngest deities in Greek mythology—of the main Olympian deities only Dionysus was younger—Hermes was usually depicted in pre-fifth-century-BCE art as a mature male with a full-grown beard. In sculptures and paintings after the fifth century BCE, he was most commonly shown as a beardless youth, wearing a winged cap and sandals, symbols of his speed. He is also often shown carrying a herald's staff—called a *kerykeion* by the Greeks and a *caduceus* by the Romans—decorated with intertwined snakes, which were symbols of immortality. Asclepius, the god of healing, carried a similar staff with intertwined snakes. The staff is now commonly used as a symbol of healing by the modern medical profession in North America and many other parts of the world.

The god of boundaries

It has been argued that Hermes' role as the god of boundaries (see box, page 672) relates in some ways to most of his other responsibilities and characteristics. For example, he was the god of shepherds because they try to keep herds within the bounds of a pasture, and he was the god of heralds and messengers because they travel across boundaries to deliver messages. Occasionally Hermes also led the souls of the dead across the boundary separating the land of the living from the underworld, to hand them to Charon, the ferryman of Hades. In this guise he was called Hermes Psychopompos ("soul-leader"), and he was the only god, besides Persephone and Hades, who could cross into the land of the dead and out again.

Right: British artist Evelyn De Morgan (c. 1850–1919) painted this version of Hermes with the deity appearing youthful, wearing winged sandals and cap, and carrying his staff. One of the two snakes of immortality is approaching the staff to intertwine with the other. De Morgan titled the painting Mercury, *using the Roman name for Hermes.*

Hermes and Herms

In recognition of Hermes' role as god of boundaries, the ancient Greeks built herms, named in honor of the god. Herms were stone square pillars placed at the boundary between properties or at crossroads. Many herms were crowned with a bust of the god or other mythological characters, and some had an erect phallus on the pillar. In addition to their practical purpose of demarcating the boundary, herms were thought to bring good luck.

One legend has it that herms were formerly people who had angered Hermes and as punishment had been transformed into the stone pillars. Cursed to stand at a boundary forever, the victim would be forced to observe everyone who passed, but would be unable to prevent their passing or to tell anyone later who had gone by.

Herms had great religious significance and were common in classical times. When most of the herms in Athens were mutilated one night shortly before a major military expedition against Sicily, it was thought that war protesters were casting bad omens. The men who were held responsible for the crime, including Alcibiades (c. 450–404 BCE), the leader of the expedition, were put on trial or forced into exile.

Above: This ancient Greek herm was built at the boundary of a theater in what is now Libya. The bust of a satyr, perhaps in recognition of Hermes' son Pan, is mounted on top.

Another of Hermes' responsibilities was to watch over the safe passage of a bride from her father's house to her new husband's on her wedding day. According to Hesiod, a Greek poet who lived around 800 BCE, Hermes would give the bride the soft words with which she could win her new husband's love.

Similar deities in other cultures

Several of Hermes' characteristics have parallels in West Asian and Indo-European myth. Hittite gods and their messengers, for instance, were described as "wearing the winds as shoes" when they set out on their journeys. Hermes wore winged sandals, which, according to Homer, enabled him to travel "as swiftly as the blowing winds." The intertwined snakes on Hermes' staff also appear in the traditions of ancient West Asian cultures. Hermes' equivalent in Indo-European tradition is the Indic god Pushan, who appears in the Rig Veda, the earliest of the Sanskrit sacred texts, written around 1500 BCE. Like Hermes, Pushan was a god of herds, a messenger, and a traveler. Pushan was also involved in marriage as the god who prepared a new bride for her husband.

Hermes tricks Apollo

The longest myth told about Hermes is found in "Hymn to Hermes," a poem composed by an anonymous Greek oral poet, probably at the end of the sixth century BCE, although some scholars attribute its authorship to Homer. This myth tells the story of the first two days of Hermes' life. "Born at dawn," it tells us, "at midday he played the lyre, and in the evening he stole the cattle of the far-shooting Apollo." The hymn goes on to describe Hermes as a "wily child, a thief, a cattle driver, a dream bringer, and a night watcher." The myth shows Hermes' nature as a trickster, a figure common in many mythologies who can be both helpful and destructive, trustworthy and deceitful.

According to the hymn, Hermes was born in a cave on Mount Cyllene, where his mother, Maia, lived. Maia was either a nymph or one of the seven Pleiades, daughters of the Titan Atlas. Shortly after his birth, Hermes climbed out of his cradle and left the cave to steal the cattle of his older brother, Apollo. Just outside the door, he caught sight of a tortoise, which he killed. He took the tortoiseshell and strung it with catgut to make a lyre. He then set out for the meadows where Apollo pastured his cattle, in Pieria, more than 150 miles (240 km) away, and arrived at sunset.

Hermes stole 50 cows and drove them backward to confuse their route. According to Hesiod, he tied brushwood to the cows' tails to brush away their footprints

Left: French artist Claude Lorrain (1600–1682) based this painting on the "Hymn to Hermes." In the painting Apollo, at left, guards a herd of cattle, but while his back is turned Hermes steals the cows.

as they walked; another legend has it that he put sandals on the cattle to deceive Apollo. He also wore sandals to obscure his own footprints. He drove the cattle into a cave near his home, where he butchered two of the cattle, roasted the meat, and divided it into 12 equal portions as a symbolic sacrifice for each of the Olympian gods, including himself. Afterward he crept home, slid into his mother's cave on Mount Cyllene, and lay back down in his cradle.

When the angry Apollo arrived at the cave to demand his cattle back, Hermes said that he was only a baby and did not know what cows were. His exasperated elder brother took him to Olympus to face the judgment of Zeus. Zeus was amused at Hermes' exploits, but commanded him to guide Apollo to his cattle. Once Hermes had shown Apollo where the cattle were hidden, he soothed Apollo by playing a tune on the tortoiseshell lyre. He also sang a song about the origins of the gods.

Apollo, the god of music, offered to take the lyre as recompense for the theft of the cows. Hermes agreed, and then as a replacement for the lyre he invented the panpipes.

Protector of children

In several myths Hermes was entrusted with the protection of children, carrying them away from danger. According to Apollodorus, a Greek writer who collected and recorded myths in the second century BCE, Hermes took Dionysus from Zeus after his birth and brought him to his nursemaid, Ino, and later to the nymphs who raised him. Dionysus's mother was Semele, and Zeus did not want his wife, Hera, who was often jealous of Zeus's affairs, to find the newborn infant, so Hermes did all of this in secret.

In another episode Hermes rescued Asclepius, who became the god of medicine, from his mother's womb on the funeral pyre and brought him to Apollo to raise. In

673

other examples, Hermes did not carry the children but instead provided them with modes of transport. For instance, he sent a flying golden ram to rescue the children Phrixus and Helle, who were about to be killed by their stepmother.

In his role as guide, Hermes was said to have led the three goddesses Hera, Athena, and Aphrodite to the competition where they were judged by Paris for the prize of being the most beautiful, the event that instigated the Trojan War. Hermes also led the goddess Persephone back from Hades. According to Apollodorus, Hermes guided the hero Perseus to the Phorcides, old women who could tell him where to find the Gorgon Medusa, whom he had been sent to kill.

Children of Hermes

Hermes had several children, and his most famous included Hermaphroditus, his son by the goddess Aphrodite. Hermaphroditus was extremely beautiful, and a nymph named Salmacis fell in love with him. One day she clasped him tightly to her body and prayed to the gods

Right: The most famous surviving statue by the greatest of all Greek sculptors, Praxiteles, is of Hermes holding the baby Dionysus. It was carved during the mid-fourth century BCE.

that they never be separated. The gods heard her prayer and joined their two bodies together so that they became one person, part male and part female. It is from this myth that the word *hermaphrodite* comes.

Some ancient sources say that Hermes was the father of the god Pan by the mortal Penelope, wife of the Greek hero Odysseus, as well as of Autolycus, Odysseus's

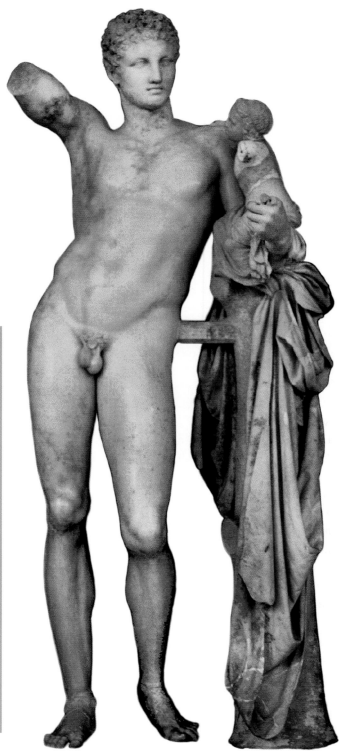

Hermes the Thief

Hermes was not only useful to the gods as a messenger, he was also a wily thief who both helped and hindered them. His best-known exploit was the theft of Io. Zeus fell in love with the mortal Io and disguised her as a cow to hide her from his jealous wife, Hera, but Hera promptly asked for the beautiful heifer as a gift, which Zeus could not deny her without arousing suspicion. Hera then put Io under the guard of the hundred-eyed giant Argus; only half of those eyes slept at one time. Zeus ordered Hermes to steal Io away, and Hermes put all of Argus's eyes to sleep by playing the panpipes. He then killed Argus, for which he was given the often-used title Argeiphontes, which means "Argus killer".

Hermes' skill as a thief was useful to the gods at other times as well. According to Apollodorus, when the sinews of Zeus's legs were stolen by the giant monster Typhon, who was trying to take control of Mount Olympus, Hermes helped to retrieve them. Another example, told by Homer, came when the god Ares was imprisoned by the twin giants Otus and Ephialtes in a brass pot. Hermes used his skill and cunning at thieving to rescue Ares.

Right: This ancient Greek pottery painting depicts a bearded Hermes with a dog disguised as a pig. The story from which the scene comes has been lost, but, as with most Hermes myths, it probably refers to an incident when he was either guiding the canine to safety or stealing it.

grandfather. Another offspring, according to the writer Pausanias (143–176 CE), was Cephalus, by the Athenian princess Herse. When he grew up, Cephalus was brought by Eos, goddess of the dawn, to Mount Olympus, where he became her lover. Hermes was also said to be the father of Eleusis, for whom the Greek city was named.

For many centuries Hermes has been a favorite subject of great artists. One of the first was Praxiteles, a great Greek sculptor of the fourth century BCE, whose statue of Hermes holding the baby Dionysus is a masterpiece of antiquity. Some famous painters who used Hermes—or Mercury—as a subject include Peter Paul Rubens (1577–1640) and Diego Velázquez (1599–1660), both of whom painted versions of Argus and Mercury (see box, page 674).

Worship of Hermes

Little is known about the worship of Hermes. Herodotus, a Greek historian who lived during the fifth century BCE, believed that the practice of carving images of Hermes with an erect phallus began with the early Greeks known as Pelasgians. He based this on a sacred story told to initiates in the mystery religion of Samothrace. There is, however, no archaeological evidence to support this claim.

Hermes was frequently invoked on curse tablets. These were tablets asking a god or gods to curse someone, which would be hidden in the grave of a recently deceased person so that the spirit of the dead could carry the curse with them to the underworld. Because Hermes was the god who led the souls of the dead to the underworld, he was an appropriate god to invoke in a curse.

Hermes was occasionally associated with oracles. In the marketplace of the Greek town of Pharae there was a statue of Hermes where, historians believe, it was common practice for a worshiper to whisper a question into the ear of the statue. The worshiper then blocked his own ears until he left the marketplace; outside the area he took the first words he heard as the divine answer to his question.

Because Hermes was the god of boundary-crossing, he was also seen as the god of exchanges of goods and of commerce. Statues to Hermes were frequently found in marketplaces, and today an image of Mercury (Hermes) is the central figure in the pediment above the doors of the New York Stock Exchange.

LAUREL BOWMAN

Bibliography

Calame, Claude, and Daniel W. Berman, trans. *Myth and History in Ancient Greece.* Princeton, NJ: Princeton University Press, 2003.

Graves, Robert. *The Greek Myths.* New York: Penguin Books, 1993.

West, Martin L., ed. *Homeric Myths, Homeric Apocrypha, Lives of Homer.* Cambridge, MA: Loeb Classical Library, 2003.

SEE ALSO: Aphrodite; Apollo; Dionysus; Eos; Hera; Mercury; Pan; Paris; Persephone; Perseus; Zeus.

HERMÓD

In Scandinavian mythology Hermód is portrayed mostly as a human hero, but according to 13th-century Icelandic writer Snorri Sturluson, Hermód was a god, the son of Odin and the brother of Balder. Hermód's name means "warlike courage."

Below: This medieval manuscript depicts Hermód on Sleipnir at the gates of the underworld, pleading for the return of his brother Balder.

Hermód, according to scholars of Norse mythology, was one of the sons of Odin—the most powerful of the Aesir (Old Norse deities). He was first mentioned in *Hákonarmál*, a poetic eulogy, or funeral praise-poem, for King Hákon the Good of Norway. *Hákonarmál* was written by Eyvind, a 10th-century skald, and in the poem both Hermód and Bragi, a mythological figure associated with poetry, were ordered by Odin to greet the recently deceased heroes as they arrived in Valhalla. Valhalla was the divine hall where slain heroes were nourished in preparation for Ragnarok, the final battle of the gods.

Yet in the poem, Eyvind does not state that either Hermód or Bragi were gods, and there is a suggestion that both may have been nondivine. Scholars have pointed out that the role of greeting dead heroes at Valhalla was usually given to heroes who were not divine, such as Sigmund and Sinfjötli, as happens in the slightly earlier poem *Eiríksmál* (c. 954), the author of which is unknown. Other examples of Hermód's nondivine status can be found in the works of 11th-century skaldic poet Pórd Mauraskáld and in *Hyndluljód*, an anonymous poem that is believed to date from the 12th century.

However, Hermód was identified as a god in the *Prose Edda*, a mythological guidebook written around 1220 by Snorri Sturluson (1179–1241). Hermód also appeared in a poetic list of gods at the end of *Skáldskaparmál*, a chapter from Snorri Sturluson's treatise on poetry entitled *Snorra Edda*, and in the anonymous *Málsháttakvædi*, meaning "Proverb Poem." Some scholars believe that Hermód might originally have been a legendary human hero who was reinterpreted as a god by the poets of the later 12th century. Also the name Heremod appears in the Old English royal genealogies among the descendants of Woden (Odin). Heremod was said to be father of Sceaf. In the Old English poem *Beowulf*, another Heremod was a Danish king who suffered exile because of his ferocity and meanness; he also undertook long journeys.

Journey to the underworld

The most famous Norse myth involving Hermód is that of his journey to the underworld to beg Hel, goddess of the underworld (also called Hel), to release his brother Balder. Balder was beautifully handsome and loved by nearly all the gods, especially by his father, Odin. Only one god did not feel so warmly toward Balder. Loki, a spiteful, cunning deity, tricked the blind god Höd into killing Balder with a sprig of mistletoe. Overcome with grief, Balder's mother, Frigga, asked the gods for a volunteer to ride to Hel to plead for the release of Balder in exchange for ransom. Hermód volunteered and immediately set off for the underworld. Hermód's steed for the journey was Odin's eight-legged horse, Sleipnir.

Hermód in Hel

After nine nights Hermód arrived at the river Gjöll, which means "loud noise." Gjöll was the river closest to the fence around the realm of the dead. (In world mythologies rivers often formed a threshold between the world of the living and the underworld.) The bridge spanning the river was called Gjallarbrú ("bridge over the river Gjöll"). Snorri Sturluson described Gjallarbrú as glittering with gold. At the bridge, Hermód encountered a giant maid named Módgud. She represents the archetypal figure who guards the passage between the two worlds.

Módgud asked Hermód about his lineage and the purpose of his journey. She said that the noise he was making crossing the bridge was as loud as that made the day before by five battalions of dead men. Because of this and because of the color of his complexion, she concluded that he was not dead. Having told her the purpose of his quest, Hermód rode to the gates of Hel and jumped over them on Sleipnir. At Hel's hall he saw Balder sitting in a seat of honor.

The following morning Hermód told Hel of his errand. She agreed to release Balder on condition that every living creature, all the dead, and all inanimate objects wept for Balder. Hermód returned to Asgard, home of the Aesir, and informed the gods of Hel's terms. They quickly sent messengers throughout the world, and everyone and everything began to mourn for Balder. Only one giantess called Thökk refused. This giantess was actually Loki in disguise, and because of his refusal to cry, Hel did not release Balder.

The myth of Hermód's ride to Hel appears only in the *Prose Edda*. The other sources concerning Balder's funeral do not mention it at all. There are, however, other Norse myths with the motif of a journey to the underworld. In one, Odin sought a dead prophetess. In another, the Valkyrie Brynhild, who had died on the funeral pyre of her beloved Sigurd, rode to Hel on a wagon following her death.

DONATA KICK

Above: This late-19th-century illustration by English artist George Percy Jacomb-Hood depicts the moment when Hermód says farewell to Balder before making the long journey back to Asgard. Contrary to the legend, the artist does not have Hermód riding Sleipnir, Odin's eight-legged horse.

Bibliography

Davidson, H. R. Ellis. *Myths and Symbols in Pagan Europe: Early Scandinavian and Celtic Religions.* Syracuse, NY: Syracuse University Press, 1989.

Guerber, Helene A. *Myths of the Norsemen: From the Eddas and Sagas.* New York: Dover Publications, 1992.

Orchard, Andy. *Cassell's Dictionary of Norse Myth and Legend.* London: Cassell, 2003.

Page, R. I. *Norse Myths.* Austin: University of Texas Press, 1991.

SEE ALSO: Aesir; Balder; Deities; Demigods and Heroes; Frigga; Hel; Loki; Odin; Scandinavia.

HERO

The tale of Hero and Leander is one of Greek mythology's most tragic love stories. Although a relatively minor myth, it remains enduringly popular and has caught the imagination of writers and artists through the ages.

Geography plays an important part in the myth of Hero. An exceptionally beautiful young woman, Hero, lived in the city of Sestos in Thrace (modern Turkey). Sestos stood on the shore at the narrowest point of a strait called the Hellespont, now known as the Dardanelles. On the opposite shore stood another city, Abydos, in the western Asian region of Dardania. The Hellespont, which divides Europe from Asia, took its name from a young girl named Helle. She had fallen into the strait and drowned while flying over it on the back of a magical ram, whose golden fleece featured in the story of Jason and the Argonauts.

Hero was a priestess of the goddess Aphrodite. Her name comes from the ancient Greek word *heros*, meaning "hero," which was used to describe men or women who were honored after their death. Hero dedicated her life to serving the goddess Aphrodite, making sacrifices to her and worshiping her in a temple. Since Aphrodite was the deity of love, Hero might have been expected to celebrate the goddess by being in love herself. Instead, according to the wishes of her parents, she lived alone in a high stone tower, with only an old maidservant to look after her. She kept away from boys, and also from other girls her own age, fearing that they would be jealous of her beauty.

Hero's love for Leander

According to the myth, every year the people of Sestos held a festival to celebrate the beautiful youth Adonis and his lover, Aphrodite. The festival may well have been the Adonia, in which worshipers planted seeds in shallow soil that sprang up and quickly died. The seeds symbolized the brief nature of Adonis's life, which ended when he was killed by a wild boar. Although she normally avoided parties, Hero had to take part in the festival since she was a priestess of Aphrodite. Many people came to the festival, some traveling great distances. All the young men were amazed at Hero's beauty and talked about how they would love to marry her. One youth, Leander, approached Hero in silence, showing his feelings for her only in his face and his gestures, and in this way they fell in love.

When he did finally speak, Leander told Hero that he came from Abydos, the city on the opposite shore from Sestos. He said that if she lit a lamp in her tower late at night, he would swim across the Hellespont to visit her in secret, using the light to guide him. Leander assured her that Aphrodite would approve of their relationship, to which Hero agreed. Every evening Hero lit a lamp in the tower, and Leander, seeing it from Abydos, swam across the water to spend the night with her. He always swam back before dawn so as not to be discovered by Hero's parents.

A tragic end

For several months Leander visited Hero every night, relying on Aphrodite to protect him as he battled the strong currents of the Hellespont. Then winter came, and the sea grew rougher and more dangerous, but the young couple were so in love that they could not bear to be apart for long, so Leander continued to make his perilous journey. One stormy night, when the sky was pitch black with clouds, a gust of wind blew out Hero's lamp. Before she could light it again, Leander, with nothing to guide him, lost his way and drowned. The next morning his battered body washed ashore on the rocks at the foot of Hero's tower. Seeing him lying there, Hero was so overcome with grief that she threw herself from the top of the tower and fell to her death at his side. No one had ever known of their love except Hero's maidservant.

Star-crossed lovers

Mythology and folklore are littered with tales of young lovers thwarted by circumstance—usually because their parents or society condemns the relationship—but who refuse to be separated by death. Hero came from Thrace, which was part of the Greek empire, while Leander came from Dardania, part of the Persian empire. Between 492 and 449 BCE the Greeks were involved in a series of wars

Above: A second-century-CE Roman mosaic, in Dougga, Tunisia, depicts Leander swimming, surrounded by Nereids (sea nymphs) and the heads of the four winds.

against the Persian Empire to keep their independence. This historical background suggests that neither the inhabitants of Sestos nor of Abydos—both of which stand as ruins today—would support a love affair between citizens from either city, and that Hero and Leander's love was in opposition to their societies' wishes.

Other stories with the theme of thwarted love include the Greek myth of Pyramus and Thisbe and the Indian tale of Khamba and Thoibi. Pyramus and Thisbe grew up as neighbors and fell in love, but both sets of parents forbade them from being together. Instead, they agreed to meet in secret, but Pyramus, finding Thisbe's bloody veil on the ground, believed she had been eaten by a lion and so killed himself. Thisbe, on finding Pyramus's body, decided to kill herself, too. In contrast, Khamba and Thoibi's love for each other promised to unite their clans, the Khumals and the Moirangs, but the Moirangs' chief rejected their marriage out of jealousy or spite. The lovers killed themselves and war broke out. The doomed lovers and warring families have parallels with the tale of Romeo and Juliet, which was used in a play by William Shakespeare (1564–1616).

The lovers in these stories are star-crossed, meaning that fate obstructs their love. Some writers have interpreted such myths as reminders that happiness is temporary and that death comes to everyone. Other people have observed that, by dying together when young, the lovers preserve their love for all eternity instead of letting it grow stale. They argue that the appeal of the stories lies in the universal recognition of the passion and power of young love.

Below: This painting, Hero Holding the Beacon for Leander, *is by English artist Evelyn De Morgan (c. 1850–1919).*

Lord Byron and Leander

English romantic poet Lord Byron (1788–1824) was alive at a time when many artists and poets were especially interested in tales from Greek mythology. An adventurer who traveled a great deal, Byron decided to try to swim the Hellespont himself while on a tour of Europe in 1810. He undertook the challenge along with his friend Lieutenant William Ekenhead, who was a member of the British Navy and a good swimmer. It took the pair two attempts, but on May 3, 1810, they succeeded. Although at its narrowest point the Hellespont is less than a mile wide, because of strong currents the two men swam a total of 4 miles (6.5 km). Their swim took them just over one hour.

Byron was hugely proud of his achievement and recorded it in the poem "Written After Swimming From Sestos to Abydos." He also mentioned the feat in his long comic poem, *Don Juan,* in which he wrote:

A better swimmer you could scarce see ever,
He could, perhaps, have pass'd the Hellespont,
As once (a feat on which ourselves we prided)
Leander, Mr. Ekenhead, and I did.

Hero and Leander in literature and art

The story of Hero and Leander is mentioned in the work of Roman writers Ovid (43 BCE–c. 17 CE) and Virgil (70–19 BCE), while the fifth- or sixth-century-CE Greek poet Musaeus wrote a lengthy poem about the lovers. Scholars believe that all three writers copied the story from an earlier version that is now lost.

Hero and Leander have appeared in the work of many writers and artists since classical times. In the 16th century, English poet and playwright Christopher Marlowe wrote a long poem retelling the story, and the tale became especially popular in the 18th and 19th centuries, when it was retold by German poet Johann Schiller and English poets John Keats and Lord Byron (see box, above). Meanwhile, many artists, including Peter Paul Rubens (1577–1640) and J.M.W. Turner (1775–1851), have depicted scenes from the story.

ANNA CLAYBOURNE

Bibliography

Ovid, and A. D. Melville, trans. *Metamorphoses.* New York: Oxford University Press, 1998.
Virgil, and Robert Fitzgerald, trans. *The Aeneid.* New York: Vintage, 1990.

SEE ALSO: Adonis; Aphrodite; Fates; Festivals; Jason.

HESPERIDES

The Hesperides were nymphs who, according to Greek myth, lived in a beautiful garden and guarded a tree that bore golden apples. The nymphs played a minor role in a number of stories, but their apples were of great significance in accounts of the Trojan War, among other tales.

The ancient Greeks compared the sun, when it set over the sea, to a golden apple. They believed such golden apples were produced by a tree that stood on an island at the end of the earth. The third-century-BCE Greek poet Apollonius wrote that the island was near Mount Atlas, in northwest Africa, while the second-century-BCE Greek scholar Apollodorus suggested it was in the far north. The Greeks believed that the Hesperides were two (or seven) beautiful sisters who wandered through the garden, singing to the tree. They were its protectors, together with a serpentlike dragon called Ladon.

The name Hesperides can be translated as "daughters of evening" and derives from the Greek word *hesper,* which not only means "evening," but also refers to the evening star, which the Romans renamed Venus. In some sources, the Hesperides were the offspring of the Titaness Hesperis, who married her uncle, the Titan Atlas. In other accounts, notably that of the eighth-century-BCE poet Hesiod, the Hesperides were the daughters of Nyx (Night) and her brother Erebus (Darkness, or the underworld). Hesiod's description of their parentage would make the Hesperides sisters to the Fates, the Keres (Destinies), Pain, Blame, Sleep, and Dreams, among others. In yet another version, however, the sea god Phorcys and the sea monster Ceto are the father and mother of the Hesperides—meaning that they would be sisters to Ladon, as well as to the three strange old women, the Graeae, and the three monsters, the Gorgons, who also lived near Mount Atlas. The number of Hesperides varies between accounts from two to seven. In some cases at least three were named: Aegle ("brightness"), Erytheis ("scarlet"), and Hesperethusa ("sunset glow").

Below: A scene depicting the Hesperides in their garden, on a fourth-century-BCE Greek vase. To the left of the image is the tree bearing golden apples, around which coils the dragon Ladon.

Male and female power

The tree that the Hesperides kept watch over was originally a gift from the earth goddess Gaia to her granddaughter, Hera, on Hera's marriage to Zeus, the ruler of the Olympians. Hera set her own dragon, the serpent Ladon, to guard it, before giving the magic tree to Zeus. Some scholars believe the story of the tree—originally possessed by Mother Earth, then by the Queen of Heaven, before finally passing to the chief Olympian god—reflects a transition in the Greek pantheon from female, mother-centered power to male-dominated, patriarchal rule.

In two famous myths involving the golden apples, bribery or trickery enables a man to win a wife. In the first myth, Eris, the goddess of discord, rolled one of the apples across the floor at the wedding of the mortal Peleus and the sea goddess Thetis. The apple was inscribed "To the Fairest," and three goddesses claimed the apple and the title: Hera, Athena, and Aphrodite. Zeus appointed Paris, the son of King Priam of Troy, as judge, and each goddess tried her best to bribe him. Paris chose Aphrodite, who promised him the most beautiful woman in the world for his wife—Helen, who was married to King Menelaus of Sparta. Paris abducted Helen to Troy, which led directly to the Trojan War.

In the second myth, the virgin princess Atalanta, a renowned runner, refused to marry anyone she could defeat in a footrace. However, her most determined suitor, Melanion (or Hippomenes), obtained three golden apples from the sympathetic Aphrodite before his race. As they ran, he tossed one of the apples ahead of Atalanta. The princess was unable to ignore the beautiful apple and stooped to pick it up, allowing Melanion to gain on her. He repeated the trick with the second and third apples, thus winning the race and her hand in marriage.

Heracles and the theft of the apples

The Hesperides and their apples played a significant role in the story of Heracles, in which the theme of trickery is also evident. One of the Greek hero's final labors for King Eurystheus was to steal three of the golden apples. Heracles

Left: This painting depicts Hercules [Heracles] Killing the Dragon of the Hesperides, *and is by Italian artist Lorenzo dello Sciorina (c. 1540–1598).*

had no idea where to find the fruit, but brutally forced the secret out of the ancient sea god Nereus. The sea god told Heracles that the Hesperides' garden lay near the mountains where Atlas supported the sky on his shoulders. In one version of the story, Heracles himself held up the sky while Atlas took the apples. On his return, Atlas was unwilling to resume his burden, but was tricked by Heracles. The hero asked the Titan to briefly hold the sky while he assumed a more comfortable position. Atlas agreed, and Heracles walked away.

In another version, Heracles stole the apples himself after killing Ladon. Hera honored her dragon by setting his form in the heavens as the constellation Draco, but she never forgave Heracles for the murder. The Hesperides also grieved, and in one account turned into elm, poplar, and willow trees in their sorrow over Ladon's death and the theft of the apples.

Explaining natural forces

The story of the Hesperides represents an attempt by the ancient Greeks to explain what they saw when the sun set. They pictured dramatic and beautiful evening skies as a protected mountain garden, which was usually hidden from mortal eyes but for brief moments was visible at sunset. The Hesperides were some of many spirits and deities that the Greeks believed controlled natural phenomena—a belief that linked them to other peoples and other mythologies throughout the world.

KATHLEEN JENKS

Bibliography
Bulfinch, Thomas. *Bulfinch's Mythology.* New York: Modern Library, 1998.
Hesiod, and M. L. West, trans. *Theogony; and Works and Days.* New York: Oxford University Press, 1999.

SEE ALSO: Aphrodite; Atalanta; Atlas; Dragons; Gaia; Helen; Hera; Heracles; Natural Forces; Nereus; Paris; Zeus.

HESTIA

Hestia, meaning "essence" or "true nature," was the goddess of the hearth in ancient Greece. She was the eldest child of the Titans Cronus and Rhea and, according to some accounts, was one of the 12 great Olympians. Like Artemis and Athena, she was a virgin goddess with no interest in suitors. She was usually represented either as a living flame or as glowing charcoal under a pile of white ashes. She was known to the Romans as Vesta.

Although Hestia played a minimal role in Greek mythology—she is rarely personified in art and scarcely mentioned in literature—she was of great significance to ordinary Greeks as a symbol of fire, life, hope, warmth, nourishment, and domesticity. While other Olympian deities were frequently away at war or indulging in romantic dalliances, Hestia stabilized and held together the homes of humans on earth as well as the home of the gods on Mount Olympus. Constantly present in the fire of the hearth, Hestia was important but easy to overlook.

Often dismissed by contemporary scholars, some of whom refer to her as "the forgotten goddess," Hestia was nevertheless in many ways the bedrock of ancient Greek society. Most of her worshipers were ordinary people who

Below: To the ancient Greeks, the hearth was more than the seat of the flames for warmth and cooking—it was a shrine to the goddess Hestia.

worked all day and came together as a family at night around the fireside in their homes. There they cooked and ate their food, offered sacrifices to Hestia and the house-spirits, talked, and told stories. Women especially venerated Hestia because they believed that the goddess attended to their daily needs.

First and last

The few recorded details of Hestia's early life are as follows. As soon as she was born, she was swallowed by her father, Cronus, who was fearful of a prophecy that he would one day be overthrown by his children. She fell deep into the hot center of his belly—to its "hearth," in a sense. There, motherless and alone, but unintentionally warmed by her father's body, she spent her early infancy.

Four siblings joined her in their father's stomach. First there were two sisters: Demeter, the goddess of grain, and Hera, the goddess of marriage and heaven. Next came two brothers: Hades, the god of the underworld, and Poseidon, the god of the sea. A third brother, Zeus, the sixth and youngest child, escaped being swallowed when their mother, Rhea, successfully substituted him for a stone

wrapped in a blanket. Zeus spent his childhood in hiding on the island of Crete. When he grew up, he and his mother conspired to make Cronus vomit up the first five siblings by lacing his favorite honey drink with mustard and salt. The children came out of his mouth in reverse order: Poseidon, Hades, Hera, Demeter, and finally Hestia. Together the six defeated their father and founded the Olympian dynasty.

Hestia was thus both the oldest and the youngest child of Cronus—the first to be born, but the last to reemerge from his body. Consequently she was often called "Hestia, first and last." As the goddess of domestic fire, without which no civilization could flourish, Hestia's special honor was to be the recipient of the first and last libations poured at every mealtime and feast, just as she herself had been the first and last of her parents' offspring. Insofar as she was characterized at all, Hestia was always depicted as calm and maternal in a general way—she had no children of her own, and no favorites among humankind: she was evenhandedly beneficent to everyone who worshiped her.

Virgin goddess

Unlike her brothers and sisters, Hestia had no interest in wars and steadfastly avoided taking sides in any conflict, domestic or international, mortal or divine. She also had no desire for sexual gratification—in that respect she was like two of her nieces, Zeus's daughters Artemis and Athena. Hestia demonstrated her resolve to remain celibate when her younger brother, Poseidon, and her nephew, Apollo, wooed her simultaneously. She refused to choose one rival over the other, and swore to remain a maiden forever. When

---

Public and Private Hearths

In the days before matches and lighters, making a fire was a difficult and time-consuming activity that involved rubbing flints or wooden sticks together to produce a spark. A domestic fire might go out at any time—usually by accident, but sometimes as part of an act of mourning—so the Greeks kept a constant fire in a public hearth, or *prytaneion*, in the city hall, which individuals could use to reignite their domestic fires.

When the ancient Greeks built houses, it was usually the hearth that they constructed first: the home was centered on the fireplace. The easiest way of heating a room was to assemble mounds of red-hot charcoal and cover them with white ash to keep the fire alive. The heap of charcoal radiated warmth and security without the inconvenience of smoke or crackling flames. Such a heap often represented Hestia herself; in the rare instances when she is portrayed as a goddess, her veil may be a symbol of the white ashes covering her internal heat.

When a bride departed from her family, she took fire from her mother's hearth and used it ceremonially to start the fire in her new abode. Until this was done, her house was not her home. The tradition survives today: some newly married couples light a candle together from the flames of two candelabra to symbolize the creation of a new family from two old families.

Right: Hestia, Deione, and Amphitrite. These headless statues are part of the Elgin marbles, classical Greek sculptures from the fifth century BCE that decorated the Parthenon in Athens.

Hestia and Priapus

According to Roman poet Ovid (43 BCE–17 CE), Hestia once attended a boisterous rustic festival with all the other deities, including the drunken and lecherous Priapus. After the guests had eaten and drunk their fill, they nearly all sank into a deep sleep. Only Priapus remained woozily awake. As he stumbled among the sleeping deities, his eyes fell on the fair Hestia. Clumsily, he started to climb on top of her. At that moment a nearby ass brayed loudly, and Hestia awoke. Seeing the huge, ungainly Priapus on top of her, she screamed, sending him into shock as he fell backward. Still shaken, he lurched to his feet and lumbered off. According to British novelist and poet Robert Graves (1895–1985), this was a moral tale, which warned against any attempt to violate female guests at a hearth, for they were to be considered as inviolable as Hestia herself.

she took this oath she touched Zeus's head—the same head from which the chaste Athena had been born. Hestia must have known Zeus's reputation as a philanderer, yet in swearing by his head she honored his intelligence and discernment. As the supreme god, Zeus could have forced Hestia into marriage, but he was relieved to have a deity on whose behalf he would not have to adjudicate in disputes between suitors. So he honored Hestia by giving her a place in Mount Olympus, where she was henceforth a sort of divine estate manager, and the hearth was her sacred domain. Hestia also became the goddess of architecture, and one of her precepts was that a "good" house should be built from the center out (see box, page 684).

Some scholars have suggested that Hestia's steadfast chastity might have been a consequence of the fact that, as an infant, she had been deeper in her father's belly than her siblings. Certainly, some modern psychologists have noted that female children who have been unusually close to their

fathers may have difficulty in forming sexual relationships in later life because they doubt the ability of other men to live up to their own male parent. It is possible that the story of Hestia—like so many of the other most enduring Greek myths—was a metaphor for an observable pattern of human behavior.

Hestia and Hermes

In view of the inviolability of Hestia's maidenhood, it may seem paradoxical that the goddess was often associated with Hermes, a mischievous and restless god who had many amorous adventures, as a result of which he became the father of Pan, the thief Autolycus, and possibly Eros. Yet in "Hymn to Hestia," one of the 33 so-called Homeric

Below: This painting of Hestia appears on the side of a Greek cup dating from the fifth century BCE.

Hymns composed between the eighth and the sixth century BCE, the two deities are linked. Scholars have debated the meaning of this reference: it seems likely that the poet intended to draw attention to the complementary natures of the adventurous, outgoing Hermes—the god of travel and communication—and Hestia, the goddess of domestic bliss. In mythology the two were friends but made no attempt to marry or cohabit.

Goddess of hearth and home

In ancient Greece, Hestia's domain, the hearth, was a sacrificial altar as well as a place for cooking. Thus it was the focus of both the spiritual and the practical life of the household. Later, *focus* became the Latin word for "hearth," and the origin of the French word for fire, *feu*; in English, the word has been adopted in its original form and is also the source of the word *fuel*.

Before the start of any meal, small offerings of the food that was about to be eaten would be thrown onto the fire to gain the favor of Hestia. In addition, a portion of all the first fruits brought into the house at harvest time would be offered to the goddess in the same way. At the end of the meal, leftover food and the dregs of the wine would also be put on the fire.

To reflect the fact that a town was basically a family on a larger scale, every city had its own *prytaneion*, a public hearth sacred to Hestia, where the fire was never allowed to go out. Situated in the town hall, it was more than a mere symbol: it had a practical significance as a public utility. If a domestic fire went out, householders could renew it from the central resource. When the Greeks conquered a foreign land, the first fire they lit there would be taken from the *prytaneion* of their native city, a tradition that was carried on by the Romans. This ancient practice has a famous echo today in the Olympic flame, which is carried by runners from one venue to the next.

During domestic naming ceremonies, a parent or one of the guests would traditionally carry the infant child around the hearth to introduce him or her to Hestia and to welcome the new addition into the family home.

KATHLEEN JENKS

Bibliography

Bulfinch, Thomas. *Bulfinch's Mythology.* New York: Modern Library, 1998.
Howatson, M. C., and Ian Chilvers. *Concise Oxford Companion to Classical Literature.* New York: Oxford University Press, 1993.

SEE ALSO: Apollo; Artemis; Athena; Cronus; Hermes; Poseidon; Priapus; Zeus.

HIPPOLYTE

Hippolyte, whose name means "horse releaser" or "one born of the stamping horses," was a queen of the Amazons, a mythical race of female warriors. She played a major part in the myths of the Greek heroes Heracles and Theseus.

Above: A Greek amphora (c. 480 BCE) depicting Theseus abducting Hippolyte. In some versions of the story, Theseus kidnapped Antiope, who may have been the sister of the Amazon queen.

According to Greek myth, Hippolyte was the daughter of the war god Ares and a mortal woman called Otrera. She grew up to become ruler of the Amazons, a tribe of warrior women who lived on the Thermodon River on the shore of the Black Sea. Most scholars believe that Hippolyte and the Amazons were entirely mythical, although some commentators think that the notion of a warlike group of females may have been based on the "masculine" practices adopted by women in some cultures in western Asia, including those of the Scythians and Sarmatians. However, the historical figure Alexander the Great (356–323 BCE), a Macedonian king and conqueror, allegedly encountered the Amazons and their queen during his travels.

Hippolyte and Heracles

The ninth of the Greek hero Heracles' 12 labors, which he performed for King Eurystheus as a penance for killing his own family, was to obtain Hippolyte's belt or girdle—a gift from her father, Ares, and a potent symbol of her power. According to Greek writer Apollodorus (second century BCE) and Roman poet Ovid (43 BCE–17 CE), Eurystheus's daughter Admete coveted the girdle because of its magical powers. In one version of the story, Hippolyte willingly surrendered the girdle, but Hera—perpetually jealous of Heracles because her husband, Zeus, had fathered him by another woman—planted suspicions in the minds of the Amazons that their queen had been abducted. The Amazons attacked Heracles and, in response, he killed Hippolyte. In another version, Heracles gained the girdle by capturing Hippolyte's sister, Melanippe, and demanding the belt in exchange.

Hippolyte and Theseus

In some accounts, the Athenian hero Theseus accompanied Heracles on his journey to the Amazon capital. In return, Heracles gave him Hippolyte as a gift. In other accounts, Theseus kidnapped Hippolyte and took her back to Athens. The abduction led the Amazons to march to the Greek city to reclaim their queen—they were defeated in the battle known as the Amazonomachy. Still other accounts say that the Amazons approached Athens only after Hippolyte gave birth to Theseus's son Hippolytus.

There are several different tales of how Hippolyte died. Greek poet Simonides (c. 556–c. 468 BCE) suggested that Hippolyte was fiercely jealous of Theseus's subsequent marriage to another woman, Phaedra. Hippolyte led a charge into Theseus's palace on his wedding day and was killed in the fray. Apollodorus also questions whether Theseus himself or his men killed her intentionally, or if

Above: This 1470 illustration from Giovanni Boccaccio's poem Teseida *(c.1341) depicts the battle between the Greeks under Theseus and the Amazons under Hippolyte.*

Penthesilea, a future Amazon queen, killed Hippolyte accidentally. One reason for the number of stories surrounding her death could be the confusion between Hippolyte and Antiope, another Amazon queen who may or may not have been Hippolyte's sister. Some writers suggest that it was Antiope whom Theseus took back to Athens; others, such as Greek dramatist Euripides (c. 486–c. 406 BCE), maintain that it was Hippolyte. The confusion demonstrates how, over time, storytellers could lose track of names in their desire to tell a good tale.

Hippolyte in ancient and modern cultures

The story of Hippolyte and the Amazons in general is significant because it involves the reversal of traditional gender roles. Whereas ancient Greeks and Romans saw women as silent, unobtrusive wives and mothers, Hippolyte and her followers placed little importance on masculinity—they only required male genes to further the Amazon race. Some present-day feminists have identified with the Amazons because the Amazons asserted themselves against the male-dominant world. Others point out

that Hippolyte's story actually reaffirms the power of men—a belligerent queen, who would never surrender to a man, ultimately did so and had a child with her former abductor.

Hippolyte's likeness has been discovered on temples, pottery, and sculpture fragments dating from the sixth century BCE, but she has also figured in a variety of other artistic genres. In English playwright William Shakespeare's comedy *A Midsummer Night's Dream* (c. 1595), Hippolyte is the fiancée of Theseus. In the 20th century the Amazon queen began to appear in popular culture. In 1941 she was described as the mother of D.C. Comics' newest creation, Wonder Woman. Around the same time, Julian Thompson's play *The Warrior's Husband* starred American actress Katharine Hepburn as Hippolyte. At the start of the 20th century the character of Hippolyte featured in television programs, books, and even video games.

Deborah Thomas

Bibliography

Apollodorus, and Robin Hard, trans. *The Library of Greek Mythology.* New York: Oxford University Press, 1999.
Bulfinch, Thomas. *Bulfinch's Mythology.* New York: Modern Library, 1998.

SEE ALSO: Amazons; Hera; Heracles; Hippolytus; Theseus; Zeus.

HIPPOLYTUS

Hippolytus was the son of Theseus, king of Athens, by his second wife, the Amazon queen Hippolyte. The meaning of Hippolytus's name foretells his fate: "one who is destroyed by horses." His story demonstrates the importance for the Greeks of maintaining a balance between opposing practices in life—in this case, between abstinence and sex.

The Greeks believed that over the course of a person's life there were appropriate times for chaste behavior and for sexuality. The former stage was overseen by the virgin goddess of hunting, Artemis; the latter stage by the love goddess Aphrodite. Before puberty, youths would devote themselves to nonsexual pursuits, such as hunting, but when they reached maturity they would embrace the world of sexuality and, eventually, marriage. In the most famous version of the Hippolytus myth, in the play *Hippolytus* by Greek dramatist Euripides (c. 486–c. 406 BCE), Hippolytus refused to make the transition from a chaste youth to a mature man. Like Peter Pan, he effectively refused to grow up.

In Euripides' play, Theseus sent Hippolytus to nearby Troezen in preparation for his son's rule of that city—a sign that Theseus considered Hippolytus to be entering adulthood with all its responsibilities. However, in an act of adolescent rebellion, Hippolytus refused to acknowledge his maturity. He clung to his solitary hunts and his favor with Artemis, and he failed to worship Aphrodite. The love goddess was therefore enraged. She caused Hippolytus's stepmother, Theseus's third wife, Phaedra, to fall in love with him when she and Theseus visited the city.

Phaedra revealed her desire to Hippolytus through her nurse. When Hippolytus angrily rejected her invitation, Phaedra became so upset that she resolved to commit suicide. Yet, because she lacked the courage to admit to her perverse desire, and because she resented Hippolytus for rejecting her, Phaedra left a suicide note, charging that Hippolytus had raped her and driven her to kill herself.

When Theseus discovered the note he cursed his son and prayed that his father, the sea god Poseidon, would destroy the young man. Poseidon sent a bull from the sea, which frightened Hippolytus's horses as they pulled his chariot along the shore. Hippolytus was caught in the reins and dragged behind his steeds. Theseus went to his son's side and, before Hippolytus died, learned about Phaedra's lie from Artemis.

A different account

In other tellings of the story, however, Phaedra is portrayed as a shameless woman who fell in love with Hippolytus but failed to seduce him. She told Theseus that Hippolytus had raped her; after Hippolytus died, Phaedra hanged herself. The mythical character Phaedra came from a family beset by sexual problems. Her father was Minos, king of Crete, who had difficulties ejaculating, and her mother was Pasiphae, who fell in love with a bull.

Below: A relief showing Phaedra professing her love to Hippolytus, on a third-century-CE Roman sarcophagus. The myth emphasizes the importance of moving from one stage in life to another.

Back from the dead

According to some sources, Hippolytus was brought back to life by Asclepius, the god of healing. He then journeyed to Aricia in Italy, where he became king and established a festival in honor of Diana, the Roman name for Artemis. Eventually he was honored in Aricia as the god Virbius, who was regarded as a companion to Diana. At Troezen, in Greece, young girls came to dedicate their hair to Hippolytus before marriage, a ritual that symbolized an end to their chaste lives and their progress into adulthood. There was a shrine to Hippolytus in Sparta, and, because of the manner of his death, he became associated with the constellation Auriga (the Charioteer).

Meaning and parallels in other myths

Hippolytus's tale encouraged reluctant youths in Greece to accept adulthood and its responsibilities, of which marriage was one of the most important. The Greeks regarded it as vital to the survival of their society, since it guaranteed the reproduction of its citizens and the growth of its cities. Hippolytus's resistance to accepted customs was prefigured by that of his mother, Hippolyte, who belonged to a race of women—the Amazons—that defied the conventions of the Greeks' patriarchal society and civilization.

Above: The Death of Hippolytus *by Flemish painter Peter Paul Rubens (1577–1640). In one version of the myth, Hippolytus came back from the dead and went to Italy, where he was honored as a god.*

Many other Greek myths have parallels with the story of Hippolytus. The mortal Myrrha, for example, scorned Aphrodite—as a result, the goddess made her fall in love with her own father. In another tale, Artemis enjoyed the company of the hunter Orion so much that she planned to marry him. However, the sun god Apollo became alarmed by Orion's relationship with his sister and tricked Artemis into killing him with an arrow. The first of these myths implies that no one should ignore the worship of deities, while the second suggests that there are some situations in which only chaste behavior is acceptable.

KATHRYN CHEW

Bibliography

Bulfinch, Thomas. *Bulfinch's Mythology.* New York: Modern Library, 1998.

Euripides, and Paul Roche, trans. *10 Plays.* New York: Signet Classic, 1998.

SEE ALSO: Amazons; Aphrodite; Artemis; Hippolyte; Myrrha; Orion; Poseidon; Theseus.

HITTITES

In the second millennium BCE the Hittites established a major empire that competed with that of the Egyptian pharaohs for dominance in West Asia. One reason for the Hittites' success was their genius for assimilating different peoples into their kingdom. A crucial part of this process was the incorporation of different gods and goddesses into the Hittite religion, which consequently developed a pantheon, or group, of deities.

Above: Carved in the eighth century BCE, this bas-relief sculpture at Ivriz, Turkey, depicts King Warpalawas (right) worshiping Taru, the chief god of the Hittites.

Between around 2700 to 2300 BCE the Hittites migrated into Anatolia (part of modern Turkey) from the north. Their language, which, like Greek and Latin, belonged to the Indo-European language family, was related to the languages of the peoples who settled in ancient Greece, India, and parts of western Asia. No one knows exactly where the Indo-European-speaking tribes originally came from, although most scholars believe that it was western central Asia. What is known is that the Hittites brought with them horses, chariots, and bronze daggers, all of which proved more than a match for the native farmers of Anatolia, who still relied on donkeys for transportation.

Between around 1800 to 1600 BCE the Hittites established in Anatolia a power base that would become the hub of a mighty empire. Kings such as Labarna I and Hattusilis I secured control of northern Syria, while from around 1650 BCE the Hittites developed their capital, Hattushash (modern Bogazköy in Turkey), which at its peak had some 30,000 inhabitants. The Hittites also developed iron-working technology, using the rich sources of iron ore in Anatolia. In the early 16th century BCE, King Mursilis I defeated the Babylonian dynasty in southern Mesopotamia (part of modern Iraq) and took its capital, the city of Babylon. However, Mursilis was murdered, and it was not until the 14th century BCE that the Hittites began to reassert themselves. When the empire resumed its expansion, it conquered the northern Mesopotamian kingdom of Mittani and subjugated the Hurrian people, whose culture was assimilated into that of the Hittites.

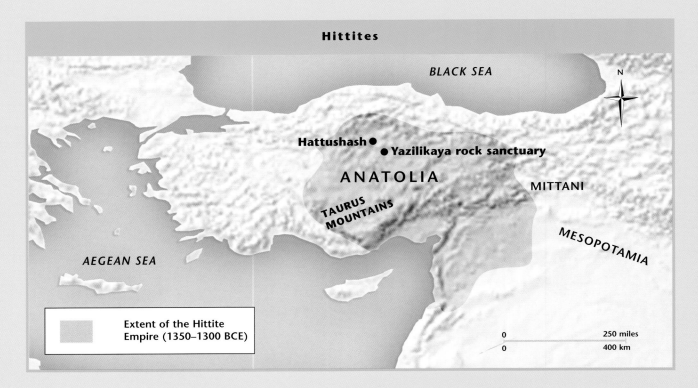

Hittites

BLACK SEA

N

Hattushash● ●Yazilikaya rock sanctuary

ANATOLIA

TAURUS MOUNTAINS

MITTANI

MESOPOTAMIA

AEGEAN SEA

Extent of the Hittite Empire (1350–1300 BCE)

| 0 | 250 miles |
| 0 | 400 km |

Through their conquest of Mittani, the Hittites became one of the two ancient superpowers in western Asia. The other was Egypt. Around 1300 BCE the rivalry between the two kingdoms led to the battle of Kadesh on the banks of the Orontes River, which flows through modern Turkey, Syria, and Lebanon into the Mediterranean Sea. Both sides claimed to have won the engagement, but several decades later they settled a peace treaty, under the terms of which the daughter of the Hittite king Hattusilis III was married to the Egyptian pharaoh Ramses II. The Hittites' power was not to last, however. Their hold over Anatolia became increasingly shaky, and by around 1170 BCE Hattushash had fallen to unknown invaders—possibly Phrygians, Philistines, or nomadic Kaskaeans. The Hittites fled south to cities in Syria, where they became assimilated into the Assyrian empire in the ninth and eighth centuries BCE.

The thousand gods

Hittite religion was polytheistic—it involved the worship of numerous gods. Indeed, the Hittites honored so many deities that they referred to their pantheon as the "thousand gods." From ancient clay tablets and rock carvings, modern archaeologists have now identified approximately 600 separate gods and goddesses. Many of the inscribed names are accompanied by symbols, such as the sun or the moon, that indicate each deity's responsibilities. However, some names have no symbols—in those cases, there is no way of telling what the function of the deities may have been. The

deities that have no surviving names are now identified by their spheres of influence. Examples include the sun god and the sea god. One deity is known today as the sun goddess of Arinna, after the Hittite town in which her cult was based.

Like several other ancient cultures, the Hittites assimilated some of the deities already worshiped by the peoples they encountered. This religious syncretism—the adoption of different deities—suggests that the Hittites were tolerant of other cultures and beliefs, and willing to incorporate new ethnic groups into their empire. This respect for diversity is reflected in the treaty between the Egyptians and the Hittites after the battle of Kadesh—the agreement is described as being between "the sun god of Egypt and the weather god of Hatti [the Hittites]."

Origins of the Hittite pantheon

Little is known about the religion the Hittites brought with them to Anatolia, although they are thought to have worshiped sky gods, including a chief deity similar to the Greek Zeus who wielded thunderbolts and was responsible for storms. Such beliefs were quite unlike those of the Hattians, the natives they conquered on their arrival in the region. Hattian religion dated back to the Stone Age and was marked by worship of the earth, personified by a mother goddess. The Hattians believed that honoring the mother goddess ensured their own well-being, as well as that of their crops and animals.

Archaeological research has shown that each Hattian village had its own deities and that, when two or more villages united into a larger political unit, the identity of each of the original gods or goddesses would be respectfully preserved and incorporated into a growing pantheon. That process continued even after the invasion of the Hittites, who assimilated the Hattians into their culture by adopting the latter's deities, often alongside their own. Among the Hattian deities who entered the Hittite pantheon were the goddess Arinna—who was worshiped as the sun goddess but may have also represented the mother goddess—the war god Wurunkatte, and Inaras, who was possibly a goddess of hunting. The mythological marriage between the Hittite storm god, Taru, and the Hattian goddess Arinna may represent one of the ways in which

people made sense of the cultural intermingling between the conquerors and the conquered.

As their empire grew during the second millennium BCE, the Hittites assimilated more and more of the deities with which they came into contact. These included various gods and goddesses worshiped by the Syrians, the Babylonians, the Luwians—whose Anatolian lands the Hittites began to rule after 1500 BCE—and, in particular, the Hurrians, whose own empire, the kingdom of Mittani, had been brought under Hittite control by King Suppiluliumas. The Hurrians were to have a greater impact on the Hittite pantheon than any other people. One reason for this may have been the marriage of the Hittite king Tudhaliyas I to the Hurrian queen Nikalmati in about 1430 BCE. Whatever the cause, the effect of the change

Major Hittite Gods and Goddesses

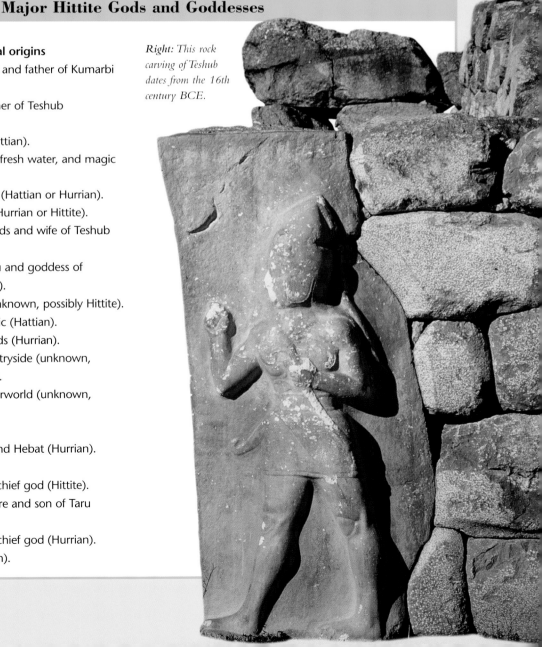

Words in brackets denote cultural origins

Alalus:	King of the gods and father of Kumarbi (Babylonian).
Anu:	Sky god and father of Teshub (Babylonian).
Arinna:	Sun goddess (Hattian).
Ea:	God of wisdom, fresh water, and magic (Babylonian).
Hannahanna:	Mother goddess (Hattian or Hurrian).
Hazzi:	Mountain god (Hurrian or Hittite).
Hebat:	Queen of the gods and wife of Teshub (Hurrian).
Inaras:	Daughter of Taru and goddess of hunting (Hattian).
Ishkur:	Weather-god (unknown, possibly Hittite).
Kamrusepas:	Goddess of magic (Hattian).
Kumarbi:	Father of the gods (Hurrian).
Kurunta:	God of the countryside (unknown, possibly Hattian).
Lelwani:	God of the underworld (unknown, possibly Hittite).
Sea God:	(Hattian).
Sharruma:	Son of Teshub and Hebat (Hurrian).
Sun God:	(Hattian).
Taru:	Storm god and chief god (Hittite).
Telepinu:	God of agriculture and son of Taru (Hittite).
Teshub:	Storm god and chief god (Hurrian).
Wurunkatte:	War god (Hattian).

Right: This rock carving of Teshub dates from the 16th century BCE.

Above: This bas-relief sculpture of 12 marching gods is one of many well-preserved works of ancient Hittite art at Yazilikaya.

was highly significant. In the rock sanctuary at Yazilikaya, 1.2 miles (2 km) from Hattushash, a carving from the 13th century BCE depicts a procession of female and male deities who all have Hurrian names. This substitution of Hurrian for Hittite names of gods echoes myths that substituted the names of the previous king and queen of the gods, Taru and Arinna, for those of the Hurrians' chief deities, the storm god Teshub and his consort, Hebat.

Major Hittite myths

Any study of Hittite civilization must give due weight to the important differences between the contributions of the Hattians and the Hurrians to the mythology of their conquerors. Scholars agree that Hattian-influenced myths were generally simplistic and served a ritualistic purpose— they were probably recounted at festivals in order to ensure good harvests or to propitiate the gods. Hurrian-influenced myths, on the other hand, were more elaborate and had less

obvious ceremonial uses. They also provided an account of the creation of the world and the origins of the gods.

Of the surviving Hattian-influenced myths, the two most important are the tale of the slaying of the serpent and the story of the vanishing god. The former relates how the giant serpent Illuyankas waged war against the gods, in particular the storm god Taru. In one version of the story, the goddess Inaras came to Taru's assistance. She prepared a huge feast, to which she invited Illuyankas. There the serpent ate and drank his fill, but by the time he left he was either too fat or too drunk to get himself into the tunnel that led to his underground home. Inaras's lover, the mortal Hupasiya, then tied up Illuyankas with a rope and left him for Taru to kill.

In another version, the serpent defeated Taru and stole his eyes and heart. Taru then fathered a son, whom he later married to Illuyankas's daughter. As a dowry, Taru's son asked Illuyankas for his father's heart and eyes. Taru, reunited with his missing body parts, killed the serpent in a sea battle. As a twist in the tale, however, he also killed his own son, who had sided with Illuyankas in the battle.

Serpents in West Asian Mythology

The Illuyankas myth is one of many examples from western Asia of an evil, snakelike creature that threatened gods or humans. For example, in the Babylonian creation myth, the god Marduk was selected by the other deities to slay the monster Tiamat. After he had killed it, Marduk sliced the monster's body in two, forming the earth with one half and the sky with the other. Serpents play an important part in two stories in the Old Testament of the Bible—one is the snake that tempts Eve in the Garden of Eden; the other is the huge sea serpent Leviathan, who is held in check by God but is destined to break loose before being finally defeated by the archangel Gabriel. The Egyptians also believed in an evil serpent, called Apophis, who hid in the underworld, waiting to attack the sun god Re on his nightly journey through the realm of darkness. The rising of the sun each morning was taken as a sign that Re had triumphed over Apophis. The Egyptians, however, did not believe that serpents were always manifestations of dark forces. For instance, the pharaohs wore the uraeus on their headdresses, a serpent that symbolized their supreme power and protected them from evil.

Right: This gold brooch from the 13th century BCE depicts an Egyptian snake deity.

was at the mercy of the malign *hahhimas*, which has been variously translated as "frost" or "torpor." Both versions of the story share a common resolution: all the gods looked in vain for the missing deity, until the goddess Hannahanna (whose name means "grandmother") dispatched a bee to help in the search. The bee found the god, stung him, and then spread wax on the sting to stop it from hurting before bringing him back to the other gods. Once the sun god was home, life on earth returned to normal.

Both myths underline the importance of agriculture to the Hittites, whose crops included barley, wheat, grapes, and olives, and who raised livestock such as cows, sheep, and goats. Unlike other parts of western Asia, the weather in Anatolia, and particularly in the Taurus Mountains in the south, could be unpredictable. The Illuyankas myth provides an explanation of bad weather and the resulting poor harvests. When Taru defeated the serpent, crops flourished, but when Illuyankas overcame the weather god, plants did not grow as well as people hoped. Some modern historians have suggested that the stories associated with Illuyankas were originally recounted at the spring festival of Purulli in order to honor Taru and ensure that the crops would grow abundantly and healthily. The Hittite story has a parallel with the Greek myth of Typhon, the hundred-headed serpent that threatened to overthrow the gods of Olympus until Zeus defeated it in battle.

The myth of the vanishing god had an even more direct, ritualistic purpose than the Illuyankas tale: there is evidence that Hittites recounted it in order to entice Telepinu back into his sacred temple, where he could once more provide worshipers with his protection. Again, this protection is related to agriculture and the seasons—the myth offers the explanation that failed harvests were the consequence of Telepinu's anger and disappearance. The myth also reflects the importance of bees and beekeeping in Hittite agriculture and society, and further demonstrates the ancient belief that honey had the power to drive away evil forces. The story is similar to the Greek myth of Demeter, the goddess of vegetation, who caused life on earth to wither and die in her sorrow at the abduction to the underworld of her daughter, Persephone.

One account of the myth of the vanishing god concerns Telepinu—another of Taru's sons and the god of agriculture and fertility—who became angry with creation as a whole and disappeared, causing all life on earth to die. His disappearance had an adverse effect on the other deities, too, who began to starve. In another version of this myth, the sun god vanished. Without his warming rays, the earth

Other Hittite Myths

Most of our knowledge of Hittite myths comes from incomplete fragments or references in contemporary descriptions of rituals or festivals. However, enough evidence has survived to provide the gist of some of these myths. One concerns how the moon fell down from heaven, which led the weather god to send storms to frighten it back into the sky. Another relates how an eagle landed in a forest, where it discovered two underworld goddesses spinning out the lifespan of a king. This myth has parallels with the Greek Fates, the three spirits who determined the lives of humans. Other Hittite myths involved both humans and deities, such as the tale of Appu, a wealthy man who desperately wanted children. Appu sought help from the sun god, who promised him that, if he went home and had sex with his wife, she would conceive a son. Appu's wife bore him not one but two sons, whom Appu named Right and Wrong. Much of this myth is lost, but it appears that, true to their names, Right respected the gods and was favored, while Wrong failed to honor the deities and was punished.

The Kumarbi Cycle

Further evidence of the influence of foreign myths lies in the assimilation by the Hittite religion of a collection of myths known as the Kumarbi Cycle, which are of Hurrian origin. The main theme of the five stories of the cycle is the struggle between the father god Kumarbi and the weather god Teshub for the leadership of all the other deities. In the first tale, the Song of Kumarbi, the creator god Anu takes control after defeating Alalus, Kumarbi's father. Kumarbi serves Anu for nine years, but at the end of this period he attacks his master and bites off his penis. Anu's seed settles in Kumarbi's stomach and grows until Kumarbi gives birth to three male children: Teshub, Tasmisu, and the Tigris River, one of the two great rivers of Mesopotamia. The first tale ends with Kumarbi's defeat at the hands of Teshub. The next three myths—the Song of the God Lamma, the Song of Silver, and the Song of Hedammu—concern Kumarbi's various, unsuccessful attempts to raise up someone to overthrow the weather god.

Below: The Sphinx Gate at the ancient Hittite city of Alacahüyök, northeast of Hattushash, dates from about 2500 BCE.

The final myth in the Kumarbi Cycle, the Song of Ullikummi, relates how Kumarbi slept with an enormous cliff that subsequently gave birth to a stone creature named Ullikummi. To protect his offspring, Kumarbi placed the creature on the shoulders of the giant Upelluri, who stood in the middle of the sea. Ullikummi grew to a vast size, overwhelming everything in its path. Teshub tried to defeat it, but in vain: he was forced to abdicate his throne as chief god. Eventually, Teshub sought the advice of the god of wisdom, Ea, who used the ancient saw that had divided heaven from earth to cut through Ullikummi's stone ankles. The creature became weak, and the gods attacked it, this time successfully. Teshub regained his throne. Scholars have compared the story of Ullikummi to the Greek myth about the sea monster Typhon.

Many scholars believe that the Kumarbi Cycle's description of the creation of the world and the history of the gods influenced the *Theogony* of the Greek poet Hesiod (fl. 800 BCE). Hesiod's account describes the creation of the earth and the emergence of the first beings, and focuses on the struggle for supremacy between various generations of deities. In a way that parallels the dynastic conflict of the Kumarbi Cycle, Uranus, the ruler of the first beings, is defeated by the leader of the Titans, Cronus, who is in turn vanquished by the king of the Olympian gods, Zeus.

The role of religion

The fact that religion played an important part in Hittite society is demonstrated by the discovery of more than 30 temples in the ruins of the city of Hattushash. Shrines and evidence of festivals have

Right: This statue dates from between 2000 and 1500 BCE and depicts an unknown Hittite goddess.

also been unearthed in various outlying Hittite villages. Ordinary Hittites had a powerful belief in supernatural forces. They attributed sickness and bad luck to either the anger of the gods or evil spirits. A variety of priests and priestesses strove to banish the spirits and appease the gods. A common way to find out if someone had angered the gods was to consult an augur, a soothsayer who interpreted the flight of birds or the entrails of a dead animal in order to determine the origin of the misfortune. Priestesses were known as "old women"; they often used witchcraft in their efforts to cure ailments. A Hittite text describes how one "old woman" cured a patient's sterility by dressing him or her in black clothes, performing a number of rituals, and then asking the patient to remove his or her clothes, an act that symbolized the removal of the evil spirits that had caused the problem.

The craft of Hittite kingship

Religion was a major feature in the life and death of Hittite kings. The basic Hittite concept of religion was that the gods were masters whom humans did their best to serve. As the most important human, the king was the principal servant of the gods, and he bore the greatest responsibility for pleasing them. One of the king's most important duties was his annual visit to all the major shrines of the different Hittite deities, at the time of the year when each one's festival was celebrated.

The king was also obliged to ensure that his own behavior did not offend the gods. When misfortune struck the Hittite empire, kings seem to have borne a personal sense of responsibility. They appealed to augurs and other holy men and women to discover exactly what they had done to upset the deities. Evidence for this accountability comes from clay tablets that record the kings' prayers, which take the form of a set of questions to the gods that seek to find out why the

Above: This bas-relief sculpture dates from the late Hittite period (about 1200 BCE). It depicts a king on his chariot crushing his enemies.

gods are angry. One example of such a prayer is that offered up by King Mursilis II (c. 1334–c. 1308 BCE), which refers to a great but unspecified plague that afflicted the Hittite empire.

Yet kingship was not all obligation; it had advantages, too. Kings could use their position as chief servant to the gods to underline their authority, especially since the Hittites believed that their kings became gods when they died. A rock carving at Yazilikaya depicts the god Sharruma—an offspring of Teshub and Hebat—embracing King Tudhaliyas IV. The carving suggests not only that the king had the protection of the gods, but also that, following his death, he became one of them. Hittite kings used religion to add weight to treaties with other states or subjects. In many parts of the empire, treaties spelled out

Women in Hittite Religion and Society

The Hittite pantheon accorded a powerful position to female deities. Both the Hattian and the Hurrian queens of the deities—respectively, Arinna and Hebat—were often granted equal status with their husbands; moreover, in the myths of Illuyankas and the vanishing god, goddesses come to the rescue of their male counterparts. The strong social position of female deities demonstrates the continued importance of the mother-goddess tradition in the Hittite religion. However, it also reflects the relative independence of Hittite women compared to women from other contemporary cultures, such as the Babylonians. Hittite society was patriarchal, but surviving law codes reveal that women could reject their parents' choice of marriage partner and, in certain circumstances, disown their sons and divorce their husbands. Hittite queens, too, had relatively strong positions. They played a role in governing the empire and retained their titles after the deaths of their royal husbands.

Right: This detail comes from a stele from the eighth century BCE that was excavated at Marash in southeast Turkey.

how local rulers could continue to lead their own people as long as they paid homage to the Hittite king, sided with him in battle, and paid a yearly tribute. These treaties concluded with a list of the gods whose anger would bear down on anyone who reneged on the agreement.

Hittite sources

Most modern knowledge of Hittite mythology—and every other aspect of Hittite civilization—is derived from the 10,000 clay tablets found in 1906 during excavations on the site of the ancient capital Hattushash. Some of the tablets were written in Babylonian, but most were inscribed in a previously undocumented ancient language, Hittite, which was finally deciphered in 1915 by Czech archaeologist Friedrich Hrozny. As well as myths, the tablets contained historical narratives, legal codes, treaties between foreign states and imperial subjects, prayers, and descriptions of numerous rituals and festivals. Unlike Greek epics, such as the *Odyssey* and the *Iliad* of Homer, the surviving myths of the Hittites do not represent a deliberate attempt on their part to record a previously oral tradition. The reason the Hittite myths were inscribed is thought to have been far more mundane: they were simply a means for scribes—the people who copied out official documents—to practice their handwriting.

The clay tablets are not, however, the only source for the Hittite myths. Rock carvings, such as those at Yazilikaya, have revealed important information about the Hittite pantheon and the influence on it of the Hurrians. The remains of buildings such as the Great Temple at Hattushash (see box, page 700) have provided evidence of how people worshiped the deities, as well as the sorts of rituals and festivals in which they participated. Finally, pottery artifacts have shown how artists envisaged their gods and goddesses. One such artifact is the pair of bulls discovered in Hattushash: historians believe the ornament depicts Seri and Hurri, the divine bulls that drew Teshub's chariot.

The influence of Hittite religion

Considering the Hittites' dominance over much of western Asia in the second millennium BCE, their loss of power in the following millennium was little short of spectacular. Over the next three thousand years the memory of the Hittite empire passed into oblivion. Before the discovery

The Great Temple at Hattushash

The remains of the Great Temple in the Hittite capital Hattushash provide powerful evidence of the primary role of religion in everyday Hittite life. The Great Temple formed the centerpiece of a huge complex, which was approximately 300 yards (275 m) long on each side and housed a variety of smaller temples, a school for scribes, and accommodation for the people who looked after the buildings. The Great Temple appears to have served three major purposes. First, it housed shrines to the chief Hittite god and goddess.

Second, it was the site of major Hittite religious festivals, which involved ritual washings, sacrifices, and libations. Finally, the Great Temple was the home of the chief god, who was given a dining room and a bedroom, as well as the services of a number of temple servants.

Below: An aerial view of the ruins of Hattushash. The city was the capital of the Hittite civilization almost continuously from the third millennium BCE until it was destroyed around 1190 BCE.

of the clay tablets at Hattushash, one of the few means by which the Hittite name survived was the Old Testament of the Bible, which records, for instance, that Uriah the Hittite was a captain in the army of King David. However, the disintegration of the Hittite empire hides its influence on the cultures and religions of subsequent peoples. Some scholars believe that the Hittite concept of a large pantheon of gods inspired the ancient Greeks to develop their own array of deities. Furthermore, the Hittite myths, from the Kumarbi Cycle to the myth of the vanishing god, find echoes in the stories that were later written down by the poets of Greece and Rome.

ANDREW CAMPBELL

Bibliography

Cavendish, Richard, ed. *Man, Myth, and Magic.* New York: Marshall Cavendish, 1995.

Greaves, Richard, et al. *Civilizations of the World.* New York: Longman, 1997.

Hoffner, Harry, trans. *Hittite Myths.* Atlanta, GA: Scholars Press, 1990.

Macqueen, J. G. *The Hittites.* London: Thames and Hudson, 1996.

Scarre, Christopher, and Brian Fagan. *Ancient Civilizations.* New York: Longman, 1997.

Storm, Rachel. *The Encyclopedia of Eastern Mythology.* London: Lorenz Books, 1999.

SEE ALSO: Demeter; Egypt; Mesopotamia; Persephone; Uranus; Zeus.

HORUS

The name Horus comes from the Egyptian word *hor*, "he who is above" or "he who is distant," a reference, originally, to Horus the Elder, the falcon-headed sun god, who was also the chief symbol of royalty. Horus the Younger, often depicted as a child on the lap of his mother, Isis, played an important role in Egyptian mythology.

Worship of Horus dates back to predynastic Egypt, before c. 2925 BCE. Gradually, Horus took on different forms. As Horus the Elder, the majestic falcon-headed sun deity, he was one of the most important gods of ancient Egypt. As Horus the Younger, or the Child, he was worshiped together with Isis.

Horus the Elder was identified with the living pharaoh. According to ritual, each pharaoh became Horus incarnate at his coronation and remained the living embodiment of Horus until his death, when he became Osiris. The king's Horus title was the oldest royal title in Egypt and, according to Egyptian scholar Jan Assmann, "Its emergence may be said to mark the beginning of the Egyptian state." The official list of the king's royal titles began with Horus and was followed by the names of the sun mothers: Wadjet, the cobra goddess of the north, or Upper Kingdom; and Nekhbet, the vulture goddess of the south, or Lower Kingdom.

In predynastic northern Egypt it was believed that Wadjet, who lived in the north's papyrus swamps, gave birth to the sun, or Horus the Elder, each dawn and received him back into her body at sunset. As creatrix, she was both his womb and his tomb. Later, Wadjet was considered to be the mythical mother of each pharaoh, the earthly Horus, which also made her the mother of the nation.

Right: This is one of the 10-foot (3-m) statues of Horus that stood outside the entrance to the first hall in the temple of Horus at Idfu.

Above: *This wall painting of Horus from the tomb of Horemheb (c. 1348–c. 1320 BCE) is a detail from a scene that depicts Horus leading the pharaoh to the goddess Hathor. Horus wears the double crown, which represents a united Egypt.*

Wadjet and Nekhbet were symbols of national unification. They were known as the Two Ladies, and their names were part of every king's official title. In predynastic times, these mothers of the sun were of greater importance than their offspring, for he disappeared each night. The mothers alone held the vast powers of time and continuity that brought about Horus's reemergence each dawn.

Some scholars believe that the focus on Horus the Elder as the most important god in the Egyptian pantheon, the rise of kings, the beginning of dynasties, and an emerging nationhood marked the shift from a matriarchal to a patriarchal culture. Wadjet and Nekhbet remained important symbols of royal protection, but as goddesses they were eclipsed by others. Eventually Wadjet became part of all Egyptian goddesses and her cobra hieroglyph had to be written at the end of the word *goddess*. From around 1539 BCE, she was represented in the form of one of the twin symbols on the headdresses of the queens.

Horus's name dates back to at least 3100 BCE, the beginning of the dynastic period in his "town of the hawk," or Hierakonpolis, south of Luxor; it may date back even earlier, since sources from the 19th Dynasty (1295–1186 BCE) call Egypt's predynastic leaders "followers of Horus." Horus the Elder gradually assimilated countless other regional horuses, each of them a falcon- or hawk-headed god. The eyes of this royal deity were the sun and moon; sometimes he was himself the sun, especially under the later name of Re-horakhty, or Re-"Horus-of-the-Two-Horizons." As this composite form, Horus was depicted as a falcon with a sun disk on his head.

Origins of Horus the Younger

The child god, Horus the Younger, became one of the central figures in the richest and most dramatic myth of ancient Egypt. The boy god was usually depicted sitting on the lap of his mother, the goddess Isis—an image that was later borrowed by Christian artists in depicting the Madonna and Child.

Horus's parents were Isis and Osiris. According to Greek writer Plutarch (c. 46–120 CE), they fell in love, became betrothed, and were married, when still in the womb of their sky mother Nut. Their sister and brother, Nepthys and Seth, were also in Nut's womb. Nut's womb was the vast night sky—she is depicted in ancient art with her body arched across the heavens while her outstretched fingers and toes delicately rest on the body of her husband, Geb, the earth. Within Nut's womb, however, there was also hostility, for the brothers, Osiris and Seth (also Set or Setekh), were engaged in constant struggles.

The Seven Scorpions

When Isis fled to the papyrus marshes after the murder of her husband Osiris, Horus the younger was born. She was accompanied by an escort of seven scorpions. One evening, seeking food and lodging in a village, Isis knocked at the door of a large house. The wealthy owner cracked open her door, saw a forlorn woman of no importance, and slammed the door in Isis's face. Isis then approached a shabby hut. Again she knocked. A peasant woman opened the door wide, bid Isis welcome, and invited her in to share her simple meal and spend the night.

The scorpions were furious at the way the rich woman had treated the goddess and her son. Six of them milked their venom into the tail of Tefen, the seventh. Tefen slipped inside the woman's house and injected the venom into her sleeping child. The mother picked up her dying child and begged the villagers for help, but everyone shut their doors against her, for they knew her mean-spiritedness. Isis heard her cries, took pity on the child, and turned time back to the moment before the poison was injected. The grateful mother gave all she owned to Isis and the peasant woman. Knowledge of the spell spread through Egypt and was used to heal children stung by scorpions.

Rivalry between Seth and Osiris

When the four siblings emerged from the womb, firstborn Osiris and his wife Isis became king and queen of the world. Instead of ruling as a king, however, Osiris preferred to wander the earth, civilizing its peoples by bringing them gifts such as barley and grapes, art, and law, while leaving the governance of the realm to Isis.

In the meantime Nepthys and Seth had married and Nepthys gave birth to the jackal-headed god, Anubis. His ability to dismember a carcass was mirrored by his ability to restore it to life. Thus, Anubis served as a guide for the dead. The honor given him was in sharp contrast to the dread aroused by his father Seth, who was associated with drought, scorching heat, and hostility to humans.

Seth grew increasingly jealous of the love Osiris received from his grateful people; he even suspected Nepthys of betraying him in bed with Osiris. Embittered and vengeful, Seth devised a plan to rid the world of his brother. He gathered 72 henchmen and had a handsome wooden chest crafted to Osiris's exact measure. Then he impatiently awaited his brother's return.

When Osiris eventually reappeared, Seth invited him to a grand banquet. Always willing to let bygones be bygones, Osiris accepted. He was witty and amusing, sharing his travel stories with everyone—the life of the party. After everyone had eaten and drunk their fill, Seth had the chest brought in and placed before his guests. Osiris and the others were amazed by the stunning workmanship.

When Seth announced that he would give the box to the first person that fit it perfectly, his guests eagerly climbed into the box, one by one. Some were too short, others too long, some too wide, others too thin. No one fit perfectly. Finally, only Osiris was left. At his brother's urging he too climbed into the box. Instantly, Seth and his followers leaped forward and nailed the box shut while the guests watched, too shocked and frightened to stop them. Seth ordered his men to throw the box into the river. They obeyed and it was carried downstream to the sea.

Heartbroken by her husband's treachery, Nepthys fled to her sister and offered her help. According to one version of the myth, the sisters found the beached box with Osiris's body on the shore of Nedit, where he had drowned.

According to a more elaborate version of the myth, the sea carried the coffin to Lebanon. After many adventures, the grieving Isis found Osiris's body there and brought him home, hiding his corpse in the northern papyrus swamps.

However, Seth learned of his sister's hiding place and retrieved the body. He and his accomplices hacked it into 14 pieces and buried them all over Egypt. In later times, any city of importance in Egypt claimed to have a relic of Osiris's body, much as later churches throughout medieval Christendom would claim to have a relic of the True Cross.

Isis set forth to gather the mangled pieces. She found them all except the penis, which had been eaten by Nile fish. She and Nepthys, aided by jackal-headed Anubis, moon god Thoth, and weaving goddess Neith, then reassembled the body in the swamps. Through magic, Isis created a phallus. Then, as the tall papyrus rustled overhead, she shape-shifted into the form of a sparrow hawk, lay atop Osiris's body, and impregnated herself with her husband's seed. That was how Horus the Younger was conceived.

Horus and his destiny
Isis kept the baby hidden deep in the marshes under the protection of Wadjet, the cobra goddess. Horus the younger was now the heir to his father's kingdom, for the resurrected Osiris withdrew from earthly affairs to rule as Lord of the Dead.

The Idfu Festival

Between 332 BCE and 330 CE, reenactments of the struggles between Horus and Seth were a popular feature of an annual Victory festival held at Idfu, south of Luxor, and not far from Horus the Elder's predynastic city of Hierakonpolis. The dramatic rituals may have been staged on the temple's sacred lake. Reliefs from the temple at Idfu indicate that a large hippopotamus made of bread dough represented Seth. This creature was repeatedly stabbed and gouged in imitation of Horus's vengeful fury against the slayer of his father. The audience may have played a role by loudly encouraging Horus's slaughter of Seth, who, for the Egyptians of that time, represented the foreign Persians, Greeks, and Romans, whose military conquests of Egypt were deeply resented by the Egyptian people. The ritual also symbolized the battle between good and evil.

Idfu was also famous for the celebration of the annual reunion of Horus and his wife Hathor, the goddess of love and music. Horus's falcon-headed boat brought a statue of Hathor to Idfu from her temple at Dandarah as part of a magnificent procession, full of flowers, music, and sacred offerings, that celebrated the divine couple's holy union.

Below: The great temple of Horus at Idfu was built between 237 and 57 BCE. It is the best preserved ancient temple in Egypt.

Although Seth had succeeded in displacing Osiris, he had a new rival—a tougher, more determined version of Osiris. As Horus came of age, the conflict between him and Seth became even more intense than it had been with Osiris. In fact, Egyptian literature speaks of Seth and Horus as "brothers," as if Horus were Osiris reborn and thus more Seth's older brother than a younger nephew.

Unlike Osiris, who was interested in bringing civilization to his people but not in ruling, Horus knew he had been born to rule—both as the horus, or the sun, and equally as one of a long succession of earthly kings.

Horus claims the throne

Horus the younger began what would be an 80-year power struggle when he called a meeting of the Ennead, the nine chief gods, and petitioned them for his father's vacant throne. Seth defended his claim to the throne on the grounds of being Osiris's only brother, as well as being stronger and more experienced than Horus.

Seth indeed had experience and mother-line rights on his side, but because Seth had also murdered the rightful ruler, Horus had justice on his side. Horus also had the enthusiastic support of his mother Isis and the moon god Thoth. It seemed for a time that the three of them would sway the others and make short work of Seth's counterclaim.

The leader of the Nine Gods, however, was Re-horakhty, or Re-"Horus-of-the-Two-Horizons." He was the original sun god, one of many earlier horuses, and was still functioning as horus, just as all the others were. The Egyptians seemed to be entirely comfortable with such coexisting, contradictory truths and had no need to reduce the incongruities to something more logical.

Re-horakhty was indebted to Seth because he protected the sun god on his nightly journey through the nightmare realm of the serpent Apophis. He felt slighted when the other gods seemed to be making light of Seth's important role and was annoyed by the haste of Isis, Thoth, and Horus. Insisting that more time was needed, he left the tribunal, but Hathor managed to persuade him to return.

Seth, seizing the advantage given by Re-horakhty's refusal to rush to judgment, then asked that the matter be settled by a duel between himself and Horus. After much argument, Re-horakhty finally agreed.

The duel

The duel was to take place in the western delta, where Osiris had been born as a vegetation and harvest deity and where he later died. Seth suggested to Horus that they each shapeshift into the form of a hippopotamus and sink deep under the waters. If either surfaced before the end of three months, the other would win. It was an ironic proposal, for Seth had drowned Osiris in the Nile and now this duel required Seth and his victim's son to survive underwater without drowning for an impossible length of time. Isis knew Seth well enough to know that he would not be trusting either to his lung-power or to the Nile's mercy to win. As the two hippopotamuses sank into the murky waters, Isis fashioned a harpoon from a lump of copper, tied a rope to it, and hurled it into the waters, hoping to impale Seth. Instead, she wounded her son, who screamed at her to free him. Aghast, she pulled out the weapon and thew it again. This time the harpoon found its mark in Seth's body.

Left: This statue (c. 1400–1379 BCE) of Isis nursing the infant Horus is made from blue glazed faience, a type of ceramic that was associated with light and rebirth.

Hemorrhaging and in agony, Seth implored Isis as his sister, born like him from the sky goddess Nut and the gentle earth god Geb, to forego her fury and free him. Touched by his appeal, Isis's heart filled with pity for her younger brother, especially since she knew her own son was now safe. She withdrew the harpoon. Horus was enraged. Seizing a huge ax, he hurtled out of the water like one possessed and hacked off his mother's head. Then he fled into the mountains with the head, while Isis transformed herself into a headless statue of flint.

Re-horakhty demanded to know the origin of this headless statue. When Thoth told him the story, Re-horakhty addressed the other gods and demanded that they punish Horus. They set off for the mountains, seeking the culprit. Seth found Horus asleep under a tree. He grabbed him, gouged out his eyes (the sun and moon), and then returned to Re-horakhty, claiming that, like the others, he had been unable to find Horus.

Hathor sensed Horus's plight and went to him. When she saw that his eyes had been stolen, she found a wild gazelle, milked her, and poured the liquid into Horus's eye sockets. The milk healed his eyes. This story symbolized

Below: This gold, lapis lazuli, and glass group depicts Horus (left) and Hathor (right) on either side of Osiris, god of the dead. The figure of Osiris represents King Osorkon II (ruled c. 874–850 BCE).

The Eye of Horus

The eyes of Horus represented the sun and the moon and were described as white and black light. The left (moon) eye of Horus was damaged by Seth and then healed by Hathor or Thoth. When Horus offered his healed eye to Osiris, it restored him to life. The image of the healed eye (the *wedjat* eye) became a powerful amulet. *Wedjat* means "the sound one." Because of their regenerative powers, eye amulets were buried in many tombs. When worn as jewelry, the eye protected the wearer and provided him or her with wisdom and prosperity.

According to passages in Pyramid Texts—prayers, hymns, and spells intended to protect the dead king or queen—the eyes of Horus symbolized food for the dead, in particular milk, bread, meat, onions, wine, beer, cake, and water. The inner form of all food was light. Since Horus was a god, to eat his "eyes"—his light—was to live. The Egyptians considered food sacred—a pathway to the divine. That is why food libations for the dead were such a vital part of burial rituals. Food was buried in the tomb. If the expected regular offerings of descendants ceased, the food depicted on the tomb walls would be transformed to supply the needs of the dead.

Right: This amulet (c. 1068–661 BCE) is a representation of the healed eye of Horus. Such amulets were believed to protect the wearer from harm.

nature's power to restore balance to a world thrown into disorder by the lust for power. According to another version of the myth, Seth tore out only Horus's left (moon) eye, which was then magically healed by Thoth. Hathor's name means "house of Horus." In predynastic times Hathor was sometimes considered the mother of Horus. Later she was regarded as the wife of Horus. Their son was called Harsomtus.

More contests

The conflict between Seth and Horus the younger continued. In one of the most famous contests, Horus accepted Seth's invitation to a banquet at Seth's house. After the festivities, the two fell asleep, exhausted, on the same couch. Seth awoke in the night and tried to violate the youth. Horus awoke just in time, reached between his thighs, and caught Seth's semen in his hand. He went to Isis for advice. She immediately understood the gravity of the situation and chopped off the hand holding the sperm, which she then threw into the marshes. Isis made a replacement hand for her son. Then she rubbed Horus's phallus with sweet oils. Collecting its emission, she secretly took the seed to Seth's garden and poured it over the lettuce that Seth ate daily as an aphrodisiac. When Seth had salad as usual that morning, he unknowingly became pregnant with Horus's seed.

Seth, still believing he had successfully violated Horus, thereby proving himself the stronger of the two and thus deserving of Osiris's vacant throne, went to the tribunal of gods and argued his case. The gods were disgusted by this latest contest, but they believed Seth. When they saw Horus they mocked him and spat in his face to show their disdain.

Horus just laughed, saying that Seth lied. He demanded that Seth's seed and his own be summoned as witnesses. The gods agreed. Seth's seed answered from the gloomy marshes, where Isis had thrown it, thus invalidating Seth's claim. When Horus's seed was summoned, it emerged unexpectedly from the top of Seth's head in the form of a shining golden disk, much to the fury and embarrassment of the god.

After more trials and intrigue, the stalemate was broken only when an exasperated Osiris threatened the lives of all concerned if they failed to reach an immediate verdict in favor of his son. Since the gods knew the Lord of the Dead had the power to do this, Horus was finally declared the rightful successor to his father's throne.

The more ancient sources say that Horus was only given the fertile delta of Lower Egypt, while Seth retained arid Upper Egypt. By the New Kingdom (c. 1540–c. 1075 BCE), however, records say that Horus was given all of Egypt and that Re-horakhty had taken Seth as his son and put him in charge of storms to frighten humankind. Seth was not punished for killing his brother or for trying to kill Horus; nor was Horus punished for decapitating his mother. This is because the gods were reintegrated into Maat.

Maintaining balance

The concept of *maat*, or divine balance, was central to Egyptian thought and religion. The gods, the pharaoh, humanity, and the dead all existed together in the cosmos. The ordered cosmos was surrounded by chaos, which had to be kept at bay. The king played an important role in maintaining this order or *maat* by maintaining law, administering justice, and making offerings to the gods; he was known as "the beloved of Maat." The concept of *maat* became personified in the form of Maat, goddess of truth, balance, and order. Without her, the universe would become chaos again. The idea of *maat* is echoed in

Below: This statue of the Horus of Pe (c. 600 BCE) is associated with Buto, the ancient capital of Upper Egypt before the unification of the two kingdoms. His counterpart was the jackal-headed Horus of Nekhen. In their role as divine guardians, the two gods were associated with the coronations and jubilees of the predynastic rulers.

numerous other belief systems. In Japan, for example, *wa*, or harmony, was central to religious thought.

Horus the younger and Seth were seen as elemental, opposing forces. Neither could exist without the other. On a 12th Dynasty (1937–1759 BCE) throne now in the Cairo Museum, for example, both gods are shown tying together seedlings of the sacred lotus and papyrus as a symbol of Egypt's unification—in other words, both gods are needed to control what ultimately supports new life. Egyptian art sometimes even depicts them as two heads upon one body.

The Egyptians had a metaphor for the mutual necessity of Horus and Seth: the lodestone, or magnet, was called "Horus's bones," and iron was called "Seth's bones." Just as the magnet and iron were attracted to each other, so too were Horus and Seth.

Meaning of the myth

Both Horus the younger and Seth date from predynastic times—much earlier than Osiris's cult. In the predynastic period, Seth was Re-horakhty's loyal companion, a thunder god and protector of the sun god during his dangerous journey through the 12 hours of the night. Later negative views of Seth may have resulted from cultic conflicts between followers of Seth and followers of Horus. The conflict between them may also symbolize the political strife between the two kingdoms of Egypt, which were eventually united. Many ceremonies connected with the king involved the cooperation of the two gods.

For example, the king's jubilee procession, called the Sed, ended with a procession to the chapels of Horus and Seth. The festival was usually celebrated 30 years after a king began ruling and then every subsequent three years. This important ritual symbolized regeneration and was meant to assure a long reign in the king's afterlife. To signify the purification of the king, both Seth and Horus were depicted pouring water over his head. Similarly, the stolen eye of Horus that had been healed and restored symbolized the crown and the restored sovereignty of the king.

KATHLEEN JENKS

Bibliography

Hobson, Christine. *The World of the Pharaohs.* New York: Thames and Hudson, 1990.

Redford, Donald B. *The Oxford Essential Guide to Egyptian Mythology.* New York: Oxford University Press, 2003.

Wilkinson, Richard H. *The Complete Gods and Goddesses of Ancient Egypt.* New York: Thames and Hudson, 2003.

SEE ALSO: Animal-headed Figures; Anubis; Egypt; Isis; Nepthys; Nut; Osiris; Re; Seth.

HYPNOS

Hypnos was the ancient Greek god of sleep, the son of the goddess Nyx (night) and Erebus (darkness), and the twin of Thanatos (death). He was usually depicted as a winged and bearded man, often in the company of his brother. He could also take the form of a mortal, or of an owl, as befitted a god who worked by night.

Above: This bronze Roman copy (first–second century BCE) of an ancient Greek statue of Hypnos depicts him with winged temples.

Nyx and her children belonged to the ancient group of deities who came before the Olympian gods over whom Zeus ruled. These ancient gods were grouped into families of related abstractions. According to some myths, Hypnos's siblings included the Oneiroi (dreams), Moros (fate), Oizus (pain), and his twin, Thanatos (death). In other versions, the Oneiroi were his sons. Each represented different aspects of dreams, and the most important of the four was Morpheus. According to some accounts, Hypnos dwelled in the underworld with his mother. In others his home was the island of Lemnos.

For the ancient Greeks, sleep and death were particularly closely related concepts, and Hypnos and Thanatos often appeared together. For example, Zeus sent both twins to bring the body of the hero Sarpedon back to Lycia. Sarpedon, the leader of the Lycians, was the mortal son of Zeus and an ally of the Trojans during the Trojan War.

The gods often asked Hypnos to help them carry out their plans by distracting other gods or humans. He did this by "pouring" sleep on the selected target, sometimes by dripping onto their temples water from the rivers of the underworld, which were said to cause forgetfulness. In an interesting parallel, West Asian myths also speak of sleep being "poured" over people.

Zeus fell in love with a mortal named Alcmene. In order to visit her and conceive a child, he wanted a long night. Zeus instructed Hypnos to make people so drowsy that they would not notice that Helios, the sun god, did not rise for three days, or that Selene, the moon goddess, moved slowly. Zeus then assumed the form of Amphitryon, Alcmene's husband, and slept with Alcmene. When the real Amphitryon arrived, he also enjoyed a night with his wife. Alcmene became pregnant with twins—Heracles, the son of Zeus, and Iphicles, the child of Amphitryon.

Zeus himself was put to sleep by Hypnos on a number of occasions. When Hera became angry with the hero Heracles and wished to torment him, she persuaded Hypnos to put Zeus to sleep. Hera enlisted Hypnos's help

Left: The Realm of Hypnos *(late 1660s), by Giulio Carpioni (1613–1679) depicts a gloomy realm of suffering souls.*

the one hand, sleep was seen as a respite from daily cares, which is perhaps why it was often described as "sweet." On the other hand, sleep was thought to be dangerous. In Homer's *Odyssey*, for example, Odysseus repeatedly loses control of his crew while asleep, and the tyrant Peisistratos reportedly took control of Athens while the citizens were sleeping. This ambivalence extended to dreams, which could be either good and true or destructive and false.

Hypnos also occupied an ambiguous position in the Greek pantheon. He was a servant of the ruling Olympian gods, but he was also to some extent beyond their control. Zeus, for example, was unable to punish Hypnos for his role in Hera's attack on Heracles.

Hypnos was not only a figure of literature and art: the citizens of Troezen dedicated an altar to him and the Muses, and statues of him were located in or near the sanctuaries of other gods in Sparta and Sicyon.

Somnus

The Roman god Somnus, whose name means "sleep" in Latin, just as *hypnos* does in Greek, shared a number of characteristics with Hypnos. He too practiced the art of deception. According to Virgil's *Aenead*, Somnus tricked Aeneas's helmsman Palinurus into giving up his post. When Palinurus fell asleep, the god pushed him overboard. According to Roman poet Ovid (43 BCE–c. 17 CE), Somnus lived under a hollow mountain in silence broken only by the gentle lapping of the rivers of the underworld. His home was protected neither by a watchdog, lest it bark, nor by doors, lest their hinges creak, but by poppies and other narcotic plants. The god lounged on an elaborately draped couch, his eyelids heavy and his limbs drooping, scarcely able to raise his head from his chest. He was attended by his thousand sons; among them were Phobetor, Phantasos, and above all Morpheus. All his sons were skilled in crafting lifelike shapes with which to deceive dreamers.

JIM MARKS

again during the Trojan War, when she wanted to subvert Zeus's plan for the war by helping the Achaeans, who were enemies of the Trojans. Hypnos agreed, provided that she gave him Pasithea, one of the three Charites, or Graces, to be his wife. While Zeus was asleep the Achaeans won their battle with the Trojans. Like many characters in Greek myth, Hypnos's affections were not always restricted to the opposite sex. He became enamored of the handsome young man Endymion and put him to sleep for eternity with his eyes open, so that the god could always look into them.

Attitudes toward sleep

The ambivalent attitude that ancient Greeks had toward sleep helps explain why Hypnos is a more complex figure than most of the other gods who represent abstractions. On

Bibliography

Bulfinch, Thomas. *Bulfinch's Mythology.* New York: Modern Library, 1998.

Homer, and Robert Fagles, trans. *The Odyssey.* New York: Penguin USA, 1999.

Virgil, and Robert Fitzgerald, trans. *The Aeneid.* New York: Vintage, 1990.

SEE ALSO: Endymion; Hera; Heracles; Morpheus; Nyx; Odysseus.

ICARUS

Icarus was the son of the mythical inventor and craftsman Daedalus and Naukrate, a slave of King Minos of Crete. He is famous for flying too close to the sun, wearing a pair of wings built by his father. Some writers have seen Icarus's fate as a warning for people to be aware of their limitations.

Below: Daedalus and Icarus, *by Italian sculptor Antonio Canova (1757–1822), shows Daedalus securing wings onto his son.*

Daedalus was Minos's chief artisan. He constructed many fabulous inventions for his employer, including a hollow wooden cow in which Minos's wife, Pasiphae, hid in order to seduce a bull. Pasiphae's union with the animal resulted in the birth of the Minotaur—a monster who was half man, half bull—and led to another of Daedalus's creations, the labyrinth in which Minos concealed the creature, but the king became angry with Daedalus, either because of his role in the queen's adultery with the bull or because he helped the hero Theseus kill the Minotaur. Consequently, Minos put his inventor in prison, along with Icarus, now a young man.

Walls could not hold Daedalus, however. He constructed wings of feathers and wax for himself and Icarus, and the two flew out of the prison and away from Crete. Before their departure, Daedalus warned his son not to fly too low, in case the sea spray should soak his wings, or too high, in case the rays of the sun should melt the wax, but once he was in the air, Icarus soared higher and higher, ignoring his father's calls. Their route led north from Crete across the Aegean Sea, where, off the island of Samos, Icarus flew so close to the sun that his wings melted and came apart, and the youth plunged to his death. His body washed ashore on a nearby island, where it was found by the Greek hero Heracles, who buried the body and named the island Icaria and the sea around it Icarian in honor of Icarus. Other accounts, however, relate that Daedalus himself buried his son.

Origins of the story

The pairing of a legendary craftsman with a protégé, or apprentice, is a common theme in a number of ancient eastern Mediterranean myths. Examples include Kothar and Khasis, whom inhabitants of the city of Ugarit (in present-day Syria) believed to be artisans to the gods, and Bezalel and Oholiab, who, according to the Bible, built the tabernacle, or sanctuary, for the Ark of the Covenant. Since some of these cultures predate the arrival of the Greeks in the region, the story of Daedalus and Icarus was probably adapted from an earlier tale. Its connection with Crete supports the idea of adaptation, since the island was home to the Minoan civilization—named by scholars for the mythical King Minos—which enjoyed extensive contacts with other cultures and was eventually absorbed into mainland Greek civilization. The technological achievements of the Minoans—including their buildings, writing systems, and works of art—may have seemed almost miraculous to the early Greeks. The myth of Daedalus and Icarus might well have been a means for them to conceptualize both their wonder at, and fear of, this technology.

Below: Daedalus and Icarus *by French painter Charles-Paul Landon (1760–1826). Some people interpret Icarus's fall as a symbol of human folly; others believe it shows humanity's desire for progress.*

Sources for the Icarus myth

The earliest known reference to Icarus comes from a pottery fragment, dating from mid-sixth-century-BCE Athens, on which is inscribed the character's name and a pair of winged feet. No surviving poem or play is devoted to Icarus; instead, information about him comes from Greek sources such as *The Library*, a handbook of mythology attributed to the second-century-BCE Athenian Apollodoros; the *Bibliotheca historica* (Universal History), by first-century-BCE Greek Diodoros Siculus; and a second-century-BCE traveler's guide to Greece by Pausanias. Roman writers also told Icarus's story: one of the best-known accounts of his death is by Ovid (43 BCE–17 CE) in his epic *Metamorphoses*.

Different authors emphasize different aspects of the myth. Ovid portrays Icarus as a young man who ignored his father's advice to pursue a moderate course and ended up destroying himself. On the other hand, Roman poet Horace (65–8 BCE), comparing writing poetry to taking flight, presents Icarus positively, as one whose fame he wishes to surpass. Historical writers and scholars have tended to rationalize the myth. According to many of them, Daedalus and Icarus did not "fly" from Crete, but left on a ship for which Daedalus invented sails. In these writers' accounts Icarus fell from a ship, and not from the sky.

Icarus in art and music

Icarus has inspired many artists. Flemish painter Pieter Brueghel the Elder (c. 1525–1569) inverted Ovid's description of laborers who marveled at Icarus's flight—instead, Brueghel depicts the youth's fall into the sea as a tiny splash in the corner of his painting, while laborers proceed with their tasks, unconcerned. The view of Icarus as a symbol of the human desire to "fly higher," which Horace emphasized, has been the dominant perspective on him in the modern era of technological advance. For French artist Henri Matisse (1869–1954), Icarus symbolized the dream of flight, while the American composer Ralph Towner (b. 1940) entitled his theme music for the first lunar flight in 1969 "Icarus." A number of aircraft, aircraft carriers, and aircraft systems have been called *Icarus*.

JIM MARKS

Bibliography
Apollodorus, and Robin Hard, trans. *The Library of Greek Mythology.* New York: Oxford University Press, 1999.
Ovid, and A. D. Melville, trans. *Metamorphoses.* New York: Oxford University Press, 1998.

SEE ALSO: Crete; Daedalus; Greece; Heracles; Minos; Theseus.

IDOMENEUS

Idomeneus was a king of Crete, the son of Deucalion and the grandson of King Minos. His story revolves around the events of the Trojan War, where he led the Cretan contingent, which fought on the side of the Greeks.

The story of Idomeneus falls into two parts, one of which took place before and during the Trojan War, the other after it. Before the start of the war, Idomeneus competed with Odysseus, Ajax, and Menelaus for the hand of Helen, the daughter of Zeus and the most beautiful woman in Greece. Helen married Menelaus, but was then abducted to Troy by Paris. Idomeneus and the other defeated suitors had pledged to Agamemnon, king of Mycenae and brother of Menelaus, that they would try to recapture Helen. Greek poet Homer (c. ninth–eighth century BCE) wrote in the *Iliad* that Idomeneus and his nephew Meriones led 80 Cretan ships to Troy. Idomeneus was one of the principal warriors in the ensuing war, and one of the few Greeks to return home after the long conflict.

The Trojan War

Idomeneus fought with distinction throughout the hostilities in Troy. According to the *Iliad*, he slew Phaestus, the son of Borus the Maeonian, before volunteering—one of only nine men to do so—to fight the Trojan champion Hector in single combat. This task, however, fell to Ajax. Later in Homer's account, Idomeneus instructs the aged Nestor to save the wounded healer Machaon from battle. Idomeneus's most fearsome fighting is described in Book 13 of the *Iliad*: urged on by the sea god Poseidon and accompanied by Meriones, he stands firm against an onslaught from the Trojan ranks led by Deiphobus and Aeneas. Later still, Idomeneus fought for the body of Patroclus, the beloved companion of the Greek champion Achilles. Idomeneus accompanied Odysseus, Nestor, and Phoenix when they went to comfort Achilles. Finally,

Above: This engraving by Luigi Schiavonetti (1765–1810) depicts a kneeling Mentor, a valued friend of Odysseus, giving advice to Idomeneus.

Pausanias and Idomeneus

Idomeneus was descended from Helios, the sun god, through the god's daughter Pasiphae. This was made clear by Greek travel writer Pausanias (143–176 CE), who described his visit to the temple of Zeus at Olympia. There Pausanias saw eight of a set of nine statues representing the warriors who rose to fight Hector at Troy—the ninth had apparently been taken to Rome by the emperor Nero. Although the only statue with an inscribed name was that of Agamemnon, Pausanias decided that another of the monuments must represent Idomeneus, because the shield of the statue in question bore the image of a rooster. The rooster was the sacred bird of the sun god Helios.

Above: The Greek fleet sails toward Troy, from an illustration in a 15th-century French book. According to Homer, Idomeneus took part in all the Trojan War's main battles and related events.

during the funeral games to honor Patroclus, Idomeneus quarreled with Ajax while watching the chariot race. In classical art, most of the surviving representations of Idomeneus show him during the Trojan War: for example, leading a sacrifice with Agamemnon, or during Patroclus's funeral games. However, much of his fame derives not from the Trojan War itself, but from his journey back to Crete.

The journey home

Like many other Greeks, Idomeneus ran into difficulties on his way home from Troy. During a fearsome storm, he promised Poseidon that, if he were delivered from the tempest, he would sacrifice the first being he saw on his return to Crete. Poseidon accepted the offer and calmed the storm, but the first person to greet Idomeneus when he reached dry land was his own son, Idamantes. There are several different versions of the subsequent events. In the *Aeneid*, by Roman poet Virgil (70–19 BCE), Idomeneus sacrificed his son, thus angering the gods, who drove him from Crete to Calabria in southern Italy. In another account, the sacrifice sparked a plague, which enraged the

Cretan people, who, in turn, forced Idomeneus off the island. In the second century BCE, Greek scholar Apollodorus related a third version of events. While Idomeneus was in Troy, his wife Meda took a lover, Leucus, who killed both Meda and her daughter before usurping the throne and forming alliances with 10 other cities. When Idomeneus returned home and attempted to sacrifice his son, a plague broke out. This event gave Leucus a perfect excuse to banish Idomeneus.

In all three versions, the story of Idomeneus is a sad one. His hasty oath to Poseidon and the subsequent sacrifice of his son cast a shadow over the reputation he had made for himself at Troy. However, a happy ending did come in the form of an opera by composer Mozart (1756-1791), *Idomeneo, rè di Creta* (1781), in which Neptune (the Roman Poseidon) released Idomeneus from his vow.

BRIAN SEILSTAD

Bibliography
Homer, and Robert Fagles, trans. *The Iliad*. New York: Penguin USA, 2003.
Virgil, and Robert Fitzgerald, trans. *The Aeneid*. New York: Vintage, 1990.

SEE ALSO: Agamemnon; Ajax; Crete; Hector; Helen; Helios; Menelaus; Minos; Pasiphae; Patroclus; Poseidon.

INANNA

Inanna was the most powerful goddess of Sumeria, the ancient civilization that emerged during the fourth millennium BCE in the area of Mesopotamia that now forms part of Iraq. She was later identified with the Babylonian goddess Ishtar and the Phoenician goddess Astarte, and was worshiped throughout western Asia for over 2,000 years.

In the area between the Tigris and Euphrates rivers, city-states began to emerge from the earlier farming cultures around 3800 BCE. One of these states was Sumeria, which formed around the city of Sumer. Worship of Inanna is evident from the beginning of the Sumerian civilization. Sumerian mythology was the foundation of the later mythologies of neighboring Assyria and Babylon and had parallels with the developing mythology of Judaism.

Changing roles

Inanna was the daughter of the moon god Nanna and his wife, Ningal. She was most often referred to as Queen of Heaven. Originally she may have been simply the goddess of the storehouse, particularly of dates—an important food source in ancient western Asia—but also of wool, meat, and grain. Her symbol was the storehouse gates, depicted as bound reed bundles. She was the wife of Dumuzi or Amaushumgalana, "the one great source of date clusters." Inanna was also the goddess of rain and thunderstorms, which provided essential grazing pasture for the Sumerians' flocks of sheep. In this aspect her husband was Dumuzi, a shepherd, who was later identified with the Babylonian Tammuz, and she was often depicted with a lion, or lion cub, whose roar resembled thunder.

Right: A detail of the alabaster Warka vase (c. 2900–2300 BCE) depicts Inanna beside her emblem of bound reeds, which symbolizes the entrance to a storehouse. The first in a long line of naked men bearing baskets of fruit and vegetables approaches the entrance.

Inanna evolved into an increasingly complex figure of beauty and light, darkness and death. As goddess of love, she was venerated for her happy marriage. As goddess of battle, she brought victory to the Assyrian armies. She was the goddess of the morning and evening stars (both aspects of the planet Venus), and as such formed part of a triad with her father, the moon god, and her brother Utu, the sun god. In her aspect as goddess of love and sex, her cult included sacred prostitution, and her symbol was the owl, a creature of the night.

Into the underworld

In all her aspects, Inanna's chief trait was her desire for power. Her machinations to obtain it were the driving force behind one of the most famous Sumerian myths, that of Inanna's descent to the underworld. She first gained power over much of the earthly world by getting Enki, god of wisdom, drunk. He was the holder of the *me*, the basic aspects of civilization, such as kingship, music, peace, and victory. One by one Inanna wheedled the *me* out of Enki. She then turned her covetous eyes on the underworld, which was ruled by her sister Ereshkigal. As Inanna

Above: *This terra-cotta relief of Inanna (c. 2000 BCE) depicts her with wings and talons, wearing a crown of lunar horns and a rainbow necklace. She is accompanied by lions and owls.*

Sacred Women

Inanna's sacred prostitutes were organized in a strict heirarchy: the high priestesses, or *entu*; the *naditu*, who came from high-ranking families; the *qadishtu* (sacred women); and the *ishtaritu*, who specialized in dancing, music, and singing. The prostitutes' sexual acts symbolized the sacred marriage between the goddess and her husband, which ensured the fertility and annual renewal of the earth. Greek author Herodotus (c. 484–425 BCE) reported that every Babylonian woman had to offer herself once in her life to any man who chose her in the temple of Ishtar. The man would indicate his choice by throwing a silver coin into her lap and invoking the goddess. The silver was given to the temple as a sacred offering.

descended into the underworld, she had to pass seven gates; at each one she had to surrender an item of clothing or jewelry until, by the time she came face to face with Ereshkigal, she was crouched and naked—the same state and position in which ancient Sumerians were buried. Ereshkigal's judges of the dead ordered Inanna to be hung on the wall on a hook as a decaying side of meat. Thus the power of death proved stronger than Inanna.

However, before setting off on her journey, Inanna had told Ninshubur, her handmaiden, that if she did not return in three days, Ninshubur should take action to recover her. First Ninshubur began the ritual of public mourning. Then she went to Enlil, the god of earth, wind, and spirit, and tried to persuade him that Inanna was too precious to be lost to death. He reluctantly declined to help, on the grounds that he had no power over the underworld, and that Inanna had brought her fate upon herself. Nanna, Inanna's father, also refused to provide any assistance.

Finally, Ninshubur persuaded Enki to take action. He created two messengers, Kurgaru and Kalaturru, out of the dirt under his fingernails and sent them to the underworld. There they ingratiated themselves to Ereshkigal by accompanying her in her constant mourning for the dead. The goddess was touched by their sympathy and promised them whatever they asked; they requested the decaying side of meat hanging on the wall. Ereshkigal offered them many other desirable objects but finally had to give them the meat. They restored Inanna to her former state by throwing the grass of life over her. However, Ereshkigal only agreed to let Inanna leave the underworld if she undertook to find someone who would take her place in death. Ereshkigal ordered a number of demons to accompany Inanna

to the land of the living. If she failed to fulfill the terms of the agreement, the demons were to bring her back to the underworld.

As Inanna made her way back to Uruk (the first major city in Sumeria), she encountered one mourner after another who offered to take her place, but Inanna could not bring herself to condemn any of them to death. However, when she arrived home, she discovered that her young husband, Dumuzi, far from mourning her loss, was sitting on her throne and enjoying himself immensely. In a rage, Inanna turned him over to the demons to take back to the underworld.

Dumuzi's sister Geshtinanna offered to take his place in the underworld for half the year. The time that Dumuzi, the god of sheep and spring plants, spent in the underworld was the period during which nothing grew, but when he reemerged, plants blossomed and the world sprang back to life. When the crops were harvested and the lambs grown, Dumuzi was forced to return to the underworld to await his sister's next reprieve.

Greek parallels

This myth explaining the change of seasons bears a strong resemblance to two Greek myths. In one, Persephone, the daughter of Demeter, goddess of corn, is abducted by Hades, god of the underworld. Demeter mourned for her daughter so deeply that she failed to produce crops. Zeus, king of the gods, ordered Hades to set Persephone free. He agreed but tricked Persephone into eating four pomegranate seeds. Since she had eaten in the underworld, Persephone could not leave it forever, so Zeus decided that she should spend four months of the year with Hades and the remaining eight months with Demeter.

In the second myth, Adonis, a god of vegetation and fertility, spent part of the year in the arms of Aphrodite, goddess of love, and part with Persephone in the underworld. Adonis was introduced to Greece from Cyprus or Assyria and was closely related to Dumuzi.

Fertility rituals

One of the regular major rituals in the worship of Inanna involved the annual reenactment of her marriage to Amaushumgalana-Dumuzi. The king of the city took the role of Amaushumgalana and the high priestess of Inanna took the role of the goddess. The king brought a wedding gift—the year's harvest—to the date storehouse, where the priestess opened the door to him. The couple retreated into the storehouse and closed the door. The king had to prove his sexual prowess to the goddess as a metaphor for the fertility of the land and the community. This ritual marked the beginning of the new year. The high priestess, or *entu*, was not allowed to have sex with any man other than the king, as representative of the god. She remained in this role for about 40 years (see box, page 717).

The later cults surrounding the Phoenician Astarte and the Hebrew Ashtoreth involved a much wider use of prostitution. Women took a special vow and made themselves available for a short or long period of prostitution, not with representatives of the gods, but with worshipers. Such women were called *qedeshoth* in the Bible. In time their acts lost their religious purpose and meaning—the promotion of fertility—and degenerated into ordinary prostitution.

The World's First Named Author

Most early writings are anonymous. The earliest writer whose name is known to posterity is the high priestess of Inanna at the temple of Ur about 2250 BCE. Her name was Enheduanna, and she was the daughter of Sargon the Great, king of Ur. Archaeologists have discovered more than one hundred cuneiform clay tablets inscribed with Enheduanna's hymns. However, none of these writings is contemporary with Enheduanna herself; most date from around five centuries after her death. Another relic of the period is an alabaster disk that is thought to depict Enheduanna, in a rolled-brim headdress and flounced skirt, performing a ritual to Inanna. This artifact is now housed in the University Museum at the University of Pennsylvania. Enheduanna's hymns stress Inanna's role as a war goddess, both defending her worshipers and bringing them victory in battle. She is the mistress of all gifts to humankind, from success in business to an active sex life.

Left: This sculpture of a goddess with a water jar (c. 1415 BCE) comes from the facade of the temple of Inanna in Uruk.

Worship of Inanna

In art Inanna is usually depicted as a warrior goddess wearing a horned headdress and tiered shirt. She has wings, and weapon cases are slung over her shoulders. Her earliest symbol as goddess of the storehouse was a bundle of reeds tied in three places. Later, her symbol changed to a star or rose.

Inanna was worshiped throughout Sumer, but her main temple was located in Uruk, where she was the guardian deity of the city. The Eanna sanctuary, or House of Heaven, is the oldest preserved temple in Uruk and the first known site of writing—archaeologists have found more than 8,000 clay tablets in the temple grounds. The temple complex includes a large ziggurat—a pyramid with outside staircases and a shrine at the top.

LESLIE ELLEN JONES

Bibliography

Black, Jeremy, and Anthony Green. *Gods, Demons, and Symbols of Ancient Mesopotamia: An Illustrated Dictionary.* Austin, TX: University of Texas Press, 1992.

McCall, Henrietta. *Mesopotamian Myths.* Austin, TX: University of Texas Press, 1991.

SEE ALSO: Adonis; Astarte; Demeter; Dumuzi; Enki; Enlil; Fertility; Persephone; Rebirth.

INDEX

Page numbers in *italics* refer to picture captions. Page numbers in **bold** refer to main articles.

DATE DUE

GAYLORD			PRINTED IN U.S.A.